HELP AND GOOD CHEER

Help
and
Good Cheer

BY

THEODORE L. CUYLER D. D.
AUTHOR OF "HEART LIFE," AND "WAYSIDE SPRINGS."

CURIOSMITH
MINNEAPOLIS

Published by Curiosmith.
Minneapolis, Minnesota.
Internet: curiosmith.com.

Previously published by THE BAKER & TAYLOR CO. in 1902.

All footnotes have been added by the publisher.

Supplementary content, book layout, and cover design:
Copyright © 2015 Charles J. Doe

ISBN 9781941281536

CONTENTS

Chapter 1

THE DAY-DAWN IN THE SOUL

Morning begins with the swing of the earth into the first glimmering rays of light from the sun. Spiritual light begins with the first approaches of the soul to Jesus Christ. All true converts are alike in two respects; they were once in the darkness of depravity and unbelief; their day-dawn began with the penitent turning of the heart to the Saviour. The Holy Spirit drew them and they moved Christward. Conversions have been very numerous lately, but no two persons have had exactly the same experience. With one person the first step was into an inquiry room. With another person it was the reopening of a long-neglected Bible, or a betaking himself to honest prayer. A third began with a resolution of total abstinence from the decanter, for Jesus Christ cannot dwell in a soul that is drowned in drink. With thousands the first step is the banishment of some besetting sin; and as the sin went out the light broke in. No seeker after salvation ever finds peace until he has renounced his favorite sins, and done it in order to obey Christ. *Obedience to Jesus Christ* is the test of conversion.

Some people are consciously converted suddenly. They can fix the hour and the place and all the attendant circumstances of their new birth. They can point to the very arrow of truth that pierced the heart, and to the precise sermon, or prayer, or conscientious act that brought the healing balm. With the majority of Christians I feel quite confident that their experience in conversion is literally like the daybreak. A faint gleam of thoughtfulness grew into earnestness, grew into penitence, and enlarged into a fuller, deeper sense of the soul's need of Christ; then as the soul came on toward Jesus, the ruddier hues of hope appeared, and some flushes of joy kindled up; and the soul discovers that the night of unbelief has ended and the day-dawn has begun. "I have come to the conclusion," said a very intelligent Christian lady to her pastor, "that it is *best for me* that I have never yet been able to fix the exact time of my conversion; I am afraid that I should trust too much to it if I could. Now I trust to nothing but to continued faith and to live in happy fellowship with my Saviour."

Too many new converts are apt to think that the dawn is enough, that they have reached a certain desired point and need only to remain there. As well might our globe pause in its diurnal motion when a faint streak of morning light is reached, instead of rolling on into the perfect day. Conversion is not a point of termination; it is a point of new departure. It is a start, not a journey. No one has a right to say, "Now I trust that I am converted; the work is done; I am saved; and I need only join the church and ride on toward heaven." This wretched mistake has dwarfed many a church member for life. They never outgrow their babyhood. Infancy is very beautiful in its place; but it must not last too long. I am charmed with the bright prattle of our little two-year-old grandson, who is playing with his toys and "choo-choo railroad cars" in yonder nursery; but that same lively prattle ten years hence would not be so pleasant. "When I was a child, I spoke as a child," said the great apostle, "but now I have put away childish things."[1] The first timid, brief, and rather incoherent prayer of a new convert in a social meeting is very delightful. It is music to a pastor's ears, and perhaps to the ears of angels likewise. Yet we should not be satisfied to hear the same prayer from him after ten years of sound Christian experience. Even Paul, a quarter of a century after his new birth into Christ, declares that he was still reaching forth unto the things that were before, and pressing toward the goal. The path of the Christian is like unto a shining light "that shineth *more and more* unto the perfect day."[2]

Progress is the law of true piety. The "convert" who never grows an inch in grace may well doubt whether he was ever really converted. And let the genuine convert never forget that as the germ of his spiritual life came from Christ, so his advance into godly, useful living will depend on his drawing closer and closer unto Christ. No amount of gaslight or electric burners can create a morning in this city; we must swing on toward the sun. So it is in the nearer approach to and closer conformity unto the Divine Saviour that a convert advances into a robust Christian. We only shine, at best, by reflected light. All brightness and beauty come from our sun of Righteousness; the plants of grace thrive only under His warmth. My young brother or sister, remember that *Christ's love to you* was an orb that beamed and burned before you ever beheld it. Christ's love turned your darkness into dawn. Christ's love to you is the unfailing shaft of light that shall stream into the valley of death-shade when you are passing over that river that hath no bridge. At evening-time it shall be light.

A rough old fisherman, who stammered in his speech, used to pray often in the weekly meeting, and one expression

---

1 1 Corinthians 13:11.
2 Proverbs 4:18.

was always introduced into his homely, fervent prayers; "Oh, Lord—lead us—more and more—into the love of Jesus—*for never was love like that.*" The nearer the old fisherman drew toward it the brighter and warmer it became; and now he stands—with certain other fishermen from Galilee—in the noonday glory of his everlasting King!

> "Love here is but a faint desire,
>   But there the spark's a flaming fire;
>   Joys here are drops that passing flee,
>   But there an overflowing sea.
>
> "Here shadows often cloud my day,
>   But there the shadows flee away.
>   My Lord will break the dimming glass,
>   And show His glory face to face."[1]

---

1 A quote from *Heavenly Love* by Ralph Erskine.

Chapter 2

THE SECRET OF A STRONG LIFE

I crossed the ocean on a powerful steamship, which weighed over twenty thousand tons, and pushed her way against wind and waves at the rate of over twenty knots an hour! I could not see the propelling force; that was hidden deep down in the glowing furnaces, heaped constantly with fresh coal.

That illustrates the spiritual life of every strong, healthy, growing Christian; his strength is measured by his inward supply of divine grace. The spiritual force and progress of a growing Christian prove that his life is hid with Christ Jesus. The moving hands on the face of my watch are the evidence of a mainspring. Happy are you if your neighbors who see you every day can know by your outward conduct that your inner life is fed by an unseen Christ.

The great Apostle describes this inner life of the true believer as "with Christ in God." The source of this spiritual life is divine; it begins with the new birth by the Holy Spirit. By a mysterious but very real process the new-born soul's heart-life is so united to Christ, so dependent on Christ, and so supplied from Christ, that the Apostles describes it as "hid with Christ in God."

As the root of an apple tree, concealed from the eye, goes down into the soil, feeling its way after earth, food and water, and drawing up nourishment for every limb and leaf, so a truly converted soul learns to go down into Christ for his spiritual nourishment. He learns to find in Christ not only pardon and peace, but power to resist temptation. He learns the sweets of fellowship with his Master; and so close is his intimacy with Christ that in times of trouble or perplexity he has only to put the question, "Lord, what wilt thou have me do?" A genuine and joyous Christian life is such an inner partnership with Jesus that the believer can say, "I live—yet not I, but Christ liveth in me; and the life which I now live in the flesh I live in faith which is in the Son of God, who loved me and gave Himself for me."[1] This faith is not a mere opinion, nor is it a mere emotion. It is our grip on Christ, and His grip on us. Saving faith means the junction of our souls to Jesus Christ. The mightiest of all spiritual forces is the Christ-faith, because it puts the omnipotent Lord Jesus into our soul as an abiding presence and an almighty power. It was no idle boast, therefore, when Paul exclaimed: "I can do all things through Christ, which strengtheneth me."[2]

Paul knew whom he believed. In the days of my boyhood it used to be said of a person who was converted that he had "experienced religion." A good phrase that; for a religion that is not a genuine heart experience is not worth the having. The poor weaklings in our churches have had but little or nothing of this experience. They joined the church more than they joined Christ. If they had ever experienced the incoming of Jesus into their hearts, and had experienced a new birth by the Holy Spirit, they would not so easily topple over into worldlings

1 Galatians 2:20.
2 Philippians 4:13.

and money-worshippers and moral cowards—too often into disgraceful defalcations of character. A steamer without coal is a helpless waif on the ocean billows. Empty bags cannot stand upright. It is the terrible experiment of joining a church without any heart-union with the Saviour, of trying to live without honest prayer and daily Bible food, of fighting Satan with spears of soft pine instead of the sword of the Spirit—in short, the experiment of trying to pass for a Christian without Jesus Christ—this it is that accounts for so many pitiable weaklings on our church rolls. To stand up against all the social currents that set away from God and holiness, to resist the craze for wealth at all hazards, to conquer fleshly appetites, to hold an unruly temper in check, to keep down selfishness, to direct all our plans, all our talents, all our purposes and influence toward the good of others and the honor of our Master, requires more power than any unaided man possesses. It requires Jesus Christ in the soul. Christ's mastery alone can give us self-mastery, yes, and mastery over the powers of darkness and of hell. This is the secret of a strong and a joyous life.

Such a life is self-evidencing. Although the interior union of a believer to his Redeemer is invisible, yet the results of it are patent to the world. They are seen and read of all men. Just as we know the supply of coal and the power of the unseen engine by the steamer's speed, so we can estimate the fullness and strength of a man's piety by his daily life. Our outward lives can never rise above the inward; he who has not Christ in his conscience will not have Christ in his conduct. In a thousand ways does the hidden life with our Master come out before the world. It is manifest in the man of business who measures his goods with a Bible yardstick; in the statesman who would rather lose his election than lose God's smile; in the citizen who votes with the eye of his Master on the ballot;

in the pastor who cares more for souls than for salary. The mother displays it when she seeks first the kingdom of heaven for her children, and the daughter exhibits it when she would rather watch by a sick mother's bed than enjoy an evening's gay festivities. No life is so humble or so obscure but it can shine when Christ shines through it. If Christ is hidden within you, let him not be hidden by you from an observing world. You are to be his witness. The sermon that no sceptic can answer is the sermon of a clean, vigorous, happy and fruitful life.

Chapter 3

A LOVE-MESSAGE TO THE SORROWING

his world is full of unhappy people; and in too many cases this misery is of their own making. Nothing tastes good to a man whose tongue is coated with a fever; the fault is not with the food, but with the disordered body of the invalid; as soon as that gets right, oatmeal becomes a relished luxury. Discontent is a disease of the heart, and is not dependent on external conditions. Paul could sing in a prison, and Ahab was wretched in a palace. Some of the most miserable people I am acquainted with are surrounded with external prosperities; and some of the most sunny-souled friends have not much property except Jesus Christ and a good conscience in possession, and heaven in reversion. A change of condition would be of small avail to thousands of unhappy people; what they need is a *change of heart*. The inward "Marah" must be sweetened.

But it is not the wilfully unhappy that I have in mind when bringing this love-message, but those whose sorrows are not of their own causing—sorrows that come upon them by the permissive providence of God. If such a word as "chasten" and "afflict" and "correct" mean anything in the Bible, they certainly mean that our heavenly Father does sometimes send troubles upon His own beloved children. "As many as I love I rebuke and chasten"[1]—"Whom the Lord loveth He chasteneth";[2] these are just as plain statements as words can make them. The Psalmist faced this tremendous truth when he said, "I was dumb, I opened not my mouth because *Thou didst it.*"[3] How that fact alters the case! It is a blessed discovery we make when we discover God's hand in any experience of joy, or any experience of sorrow. Further questionings will do us no good, for God keeps His own secrets; murmuring and rebellion will only aggravate our sorrows. God did it. Hold that truth right before your eyes, my suffering friend, until you can read it through your tears: and you will learn two things. First, you will learn that there was a divine purpose in your affliction, and there was no haphazard blunder in the stroke. Why God's dealings with you were wise and kind you may not comprehend any more than your child comprehends the inner works of a clock when it reads the figure "eight" on the clock's face and starts off for school. The child accepts the fact, and does not go behind it. The mysteries of Providence we are not able to unravel, and if we attempt it the silencing answer comes back, "Be still and know that I am God!"[4]

The other thing for you to learn is that the God who "did it" is not a blind tyrant, but a wise, tender, loving Father. That is a precious discovery; for we can bear almost anything if we are sure that love is behind it. Love never wrongs us. Love never robs us; never tortures us; never lays on us a needless load. The wondrous love that "spared not His own Son, but delivered Him up for us all,"[5] can be trusted under the heaviest

1 Revelation 3:19.
2 Hebrews 12:6.
3 Psalm 39:9.
4 Psalm 46:10.
5 Romans 8:32.

blow or behind the darkest cloud. You may say that you are terribly puzzled about your Father's dealings with you; but that difficulty arises from the narrow and finite character of our minds. Here we only "know in part"—only a fragment of God's purposes, and then we go off and question the whole. We judge God childishly—finding fault with the woven tapestries of His providence before they are finished in His loom. Remember also that you are on the *under* side, the dark side of the overhanging cloud of sorrow. While you may be weeping for a departed husband or a beloved child, they may be up on the heavenly side of that cloud, and be gazing on its overpowering brightness. Wrestle with that puzzle as hard as you will, you must be content to know only in part, and the rest of it you "will know *hereafter.*" If you will borrow his spyglass from the old persecuted hero who wrote the Epistle to the Romans, you will discover this glorious signal in the upper sky—"All things work together for *good* to them that love God."[1] See to it that Satan does not sour your heart toward your heavenly Father, or turn the sweet tenderness of trust into the gall of bitter murmurings.

I am often impressed by the different ways in which different persons are affected by sorrows. Some seem to have no rallying power after a great affliction; the wound never heals. On the other hand, trials that consume some persons only kindle others into greater exertions. "This financial gale has carried away all your spars, and swept your decks," I once wrote to an eminent Christian merchant after his bankruptcy, "but you have got enough grace stowed away in your hold to make you rich to all eternity." That brave servant of Christ repaired damages, resumed business, rallied his friends, and "at evening time it was light." Smitten down, he was not destroyed.

1 Romans 8:28.

The afflictions which are sent of God or permitted by Him are never intended for His children's destruction, but for their discipline. The Shepherd casts His flock into deep waters to wash them, not to drown them. "You will kill that bush if you put that knife into it so deep," said a gentleman to his gardener. "No, sir; I do this every year to keep it from running all to leaves; pruning brings the fruit." We pastors often find God's faithful ones bleeding under the knife, but afterward they yield the peaceable and precious fruits of righteousness and triumphant trust. It is that "afterward" that God has in His mind when He sends the trial. Affliction is the costly school in which great graces are often acquired, and from which grand characters are graduated.

How is it that a genuine Christian recuperates after being stricken down by a savage adversity or a sharp affliction? Simply because his graces survive the shock. For one thing, his *faith* is not destroyed. When a ship loses her canvas in a gale, she can still be kept out of the trough of the sea by her rudder; when the rudder goes, she still has her anchor left, but if the cable snaps she is swept helplessly on the rocks. So when your hold on God is gone, all is gone. The most fatal wreck that can overtake you in times of sorrow is the wreck of faith. But if in the darkest hour you can trust God though He slay, and firmly believe that He "chastens you for your profit," you are anchored to the very throne of love, and will come off conqueror. *Hope* also is another grace that survives. Some Christians never shine so brightly as in the midnight of sorrow. I know of good people who are like an ivory dice; throw it whichever way you will, it always lands on a square, solid bottom. Their hope always strikes on its feet after the hardest fall. One might have thought that it was all over with Joseph when he was sent to prison, or with John when he was exiled to Patmos, or with John Bunyan when he was locked up in Bedford jail. But they were all put in the place where they could be most useful.

And that reminds me to say that your sorrows may be turned to the benefits of others. You can relieve your own suffering hearts by turning the flood of grief upon some wheel of practical usefulness. An eminent minister who was under a peculiarly severe trial said to me: "If I could not study and preach and work to the utmost, I should go crazy." The millstones grinding upon themselves soon wear themselves to powder. But active occupation is both a tonic and a soothing sedative to a troubled spirit. My friend, I entreat you, don't let your sorrows stagnate; they will turn your soul into a fen of bitter waters, from which will sprout the rank rushes of self-will and rebellion against God. Turn your sorrows outward into currents of sympathy and deeds of kindness to others, and they will become a stream of blessings. A baptism of trial may be your best baptism for Christ's service. Working is better than weeping; and if you work on till the last morning breaks, you will read in that clear light the meaning of many of your sorrows.

Some time, when all life's lessons have been learned,
    And sun and stars for evermore have set,
The things which our weak judgments here have spurned,
    The things o'er which we grieved with lashes wet,
Will flash before us, out of life's dark night,
    As stars shine most in deeper tints of blue;
And we shall see how all God's plans were right,
    And how what seemed reproof was love most true.

But not today. Then be content, poor heart!
    God's plans like lilies pure and white unfold;
We must not tear the close-shut leaves apart,
    Time will reveal the calyxes of gold;

And if, through patient toil, we reach the land
    Where tired feet, with sandals loosed, may rest,
Where we shall clearly see and understand,
    I think that we will say, "God knew the best!"[1]

---

1 A quote from *Sometime* by May Riley Smith.

Chapter 4

THE ANGELS ON THE ROAD

In the narrative of the patriarch Jacob's journey towards Canaan we are told that he "went on his way, and the angels of God met him."[1] And we may be sure that during the journey of this year, we need not go out of the every day track of life in order to find God's angels. If they come to us, they will come in the ordinary path of our daily avocations. We need expect no miraculous appearances; for our humble lives run along a very plain, prosaic level. When common folks pray, it is not on a Mount Carmel; when we are hungry, God sends to us no ravens; when our faith catches glimpses of our Lord, no blazing cloud surrounds Him as on the peaks of Hermon. Yet as we trudge along the dusty road of duty the angels often meet us, even though our eyes recognize no visitant with the luster of heaven on his wings.

Our loving Father has many a method of directing our paths. More than one husband has found his good wife, more than one pastor has found the right field of labor, more than one young man has chosen the right occupation, when an unseen hand was guiding them just as truly as an angel pointed Philip toward the town of Gaza. From the hill top of a new

1 Genesis 32:1.

year I can look back over my own humble pathway and recognize turning points and decisive moments when my whole life was being shaped. No winged messenger met me such as met Cornelius, and bade him send for Peter; but an invisible divine influence had its hold upon my will, "leading me by a path that I knew not." Every Christian may recall many and many a time in his history when a supernatural power was at work upon him, or a sweet mercy met him, or a deliverance came in an hour of trouble, or a sudden joy flashed on the path in which he was toiling through the mire, or against a driving wind. We speak of all such experiences as "special Providences." But if God's angels are sent to "wait on them who are the heirs of salvation," and if they "encamp around them that fear Him," why may not angelic agencies have been acting in some mysterious manner upon us?

Our eyes have beheld no celestial visitant as Peter saw one in his prison cell, or as Paul saw one in the tempest-tossed vessel. Neither do we see our Lord and Saviour with the outward eye. That does not hinder our faith, or make His presence with us one whit less real. "Lo, I am with you," is the promise of a literal fact; if that be not so, our religion is a devout delusion. Let us hold fast to the other and kindred truth that God employs His angels as "ministering spirits" to the humblest and lowliest of His children. If our eyes were opened to the supernatural, perhaps we might behold them as distinctly as Elisha beheld the hosts of chariots and horsemen of fire on the mountain side. Very often we may be entertaining angels unawares when we open our hearts at the call of duty or open our door to the poor in the hour of their need. Our Lord may have had some reference to this great truth when He spoke of "their angels always beholding the face of His Father in Heaven,"[1] and also of the angels

1 Matthew 18:10.

as attending the pauper Lazarus up to the bosom of Abraham.

The coming year is unknown to us. We move, in fact, amid mysteries at every step. Unseen things encircle us. If celestial spirits attend us and watch us, how carefully we ought to live! If God gives them charge concerning us, how cheerfully and trustfully we ought to enter upon the journey of the opening year! When we need them most, they may be at hand. Faith has sharp eyes, and endures as seeing the invisible. Faith often wears coarse clothes and works at very lowly occupations—rocking cradles, driving looms, sweeping floors, holding ploughs, teaching poor children and nursing the bed-ridden in garret; faith foots it along a dusty road toward heaven; then let her go singing on her way, for the angels of God are keeping her company. With a brave, trustful heart, good friends, let us grasp the angel's hand; and if we acknowledge God's guidance, He will direct our paths aright till we reach our HOME.

Chapter 5

CHRIST EVERY DAY

The periodical piety that goes by the calendar, and only serves the Lord Jesus at set times and places is of very little value; it is only a perennial piety that possesses both peace and power. He is the only healthy Christian who runs his Christianity through all the routine of his everyday experiences. Some people keep their religion as they do their umbrellas for stormy weather, and hope to have it within easy reach if a dangerous sickness overtakes them. Others, and quite too many, reserve their piety for the Sabbath and the sanctuary, and on Monday they fold it up and lay it away with their Sunday clothes. A healthy, vigorous, cheerful working religion cannot be maintained on Sabbaths and songs and sacraments; every day has got to be a "Lord's day," if we expect to make any real headway heavenward. I have observed that those who try to live by fits and frames and feelings are never very fruitful Christians.

In setting out for the journey of an opening year, let us highly resolve to make it a better year than any of its predecessors, and let us adopt as our brief motto *Christ every day.* Our loving Master emphasizes the adverb in that gracious assurance, "Lo! I am with you *always.*" We think of Him as a Redeemer on communion Sundays; we think of Him as a Comforter when some terrible affliction befalls us; why not think of Him as a constant *Companion?* This is not a devout fancy, it is a delightful fact. And one benefit to us from having the continual companionship of Jesus this year, will be that every day will be a safe day. We need never miss the right road. We need never take a morally dangerous step. We never need be led astray. Our Divine Guide knows the whole pathway from the "City of Destruction" to the City of the great King. Wherever Christ clearly directs us to walk, there we ought to go. It matters not that you and I cannot see the end from the beginning. Jesus sees; that is enough. He sent Paul on many a perilous path of duty, and when the boiling deep threatened to engulf him, the Master was beside him and said, "Fear not, Paul; thou must yet stand before Caesar." The courage that quailed not in Nero's judgment-hall is easily explained by the old hero's declaration, "The Lord stood with me, and strengthened me."[1] What Christ did for Paul, He will do for you. Realize that Christ is in the truest and most actual spiritual sense close by you. Ask His direction; let Him lead you. I don't believe that when we put self out of sight, and sincerely desire to do that, and only that which is for the honor of the Master, we ever go morally wrong. He that walketh with Jesus "walketh *surely*."

My fellow believer, you may walk your daily life-journey through all this year in the delightful companionship of your Saviour if you keep a clear conscience, and a praying heart and an obedient temper. Begin every morning with a cordial invitation to Him to grant you His presence. Think of Him all the while as close by you. The busy bustle of the counting-room has not hindered the fellowship with Christ of many a godly

1 2 Timothy 4:17.

minded merchant who carried his religion into his business and dealt by the Golden Rule. I pity the minister into whose study the Master seldom enters. Many a farmer has communed with Jesus as he followed his plow until the acres had "the smell of a field that the Lord had blessed." Hard toiling and often sorely-tried sister, don't you suppose that your Master knows as well where you live as He knew the house of Mary and Martha at Bethany? You may have *Christ every day* if you wish. Just as surely as Christ met His disciples on that early morn by the strand of Galilee will He come to us. Just as surely now as then will those who love Him most be the quickest to recognize Him and the first to hasten to Him. He who is the living Truth has never broken a promise, and He did not utter an idle mockery when He said, "Lo! I am with you always."[1]

There is no journey of life but has its clouded days; and there will probably come to many of my readers days in which the eyes will be so blinded with tears that it will not be easy to see their way, or to spell out God's promises. Days that have bright sunrises, followed by sudden thunder-claps and bursts of unexpected sorrows, are the ones that test our graces severely. Yet the law of spiritual eye-sight resembles the law of physical optics. When we come suddenly out of the daylight into a room even moderately darkened, we can discern nothing; but the pupil of our eye gradually enlarges until unseen objects become visible. Even so the eye of Faith has the blessed faculty of enlargening in the dark hour of affliction so that we can discern a hand of love behind the cup of sorrow, and the face of Jesus beaming out of the gloom. We catch the sweet accents, "Let not your heart be troubled; ye believe in God. believe also in Me; I will not leave you comfortless."[2] It was in

---

1 Matthew 28:20.
2 John 14:1, 18.

a room of intense bodily suffering that one of Christ's veterans said, "I have no bodily strength, yet I am strong. Jesus comes to me in the watches of the night and draws aside the curtain, and says, *It is I, it is I,* be not afraid."

> Oh perfect peace! Oh perfect rest!
> No care or vain alarms;
> Beneath our every cross we find
> The Everlasting Arms.[1]

Christ every day! If that be so, then ought His presence not only to give us constant courage, but shame us from sin, and spur us on to duty. There are many things that we would blush to do in the presence of a child; how much more under the eye of Him who is Infinite Purity. When in the hurry of the morning hour, we hasten off to business without a moment of prayer, Jesus witnesses the petty larceny that robs us as well as Him. Are we tempted during the day to a sharp bargain, or some more crooked transaction? "Business is business." Yes, but what will Christ say? When we utter the irritating word or ill-tempered thrust, one look from Him ought to shame us into silence. Here is some poor suffering creature appealing to our sympathy, and selfishness mutters that there is no end to such calls of charity. The compassionate Jesus who did not count the cost when He bought our redemption, says to us, "Here is one of my poor children; give to him for My sake." There will not be, all this next year, a struggling church that knocks at our heart, or a hungry sufferer that knocks at our door for relief; there is not a lone widow that begs a pittance to warm her shivering limbs, or a neglected child running in rags and recklessness to ruin, but ever the same voice whispers

1 A quote from *A Hymn of Trust* by Miss H. O. Knowlton.

to us, "In as much as ye do it unto one of the least of these, ye do it unto Me."[1] That spotless, loving Jesus is by us every hour. Then how dare we play the coward, the sensualist, the cheat, or the wrong-doer to our fellow-man?

A new year is upon us with new duties, new conflicts, new trials and new opportunities. Start on the journey with Jesus— to *walk* with Him, to *work* for Him, and to *win* souls to Him. A happy year will it be to those who through every path of trial, or up ever hill of difficulty or over every sunny height, march on in closest fellowship with the Master, and who determine that come what may, they will have *Christ every day*.

---

1 Matthew 25:40.

Chapter 6

A MERRY HEART BOTH MEAT
AND MEDICINE

merry heart doeth good like medicine."[1] In the Revised Version it reads: "A merry heart is a good medicine." In a previous verse of this Book of Divine Proverbs, we read that "He that is of merry heart hath a continual feast."[2] So that the same thing is recommended to us both as meat and medicine.

The word "merry" here is not the synonym of reckless jollity; it is not the mere effervescence of animal spirits, or the product of sensual stimulants. It is the same word which Paul used when he told his temptest-tossed shipmates in the Adriatic to "Be of good cheer." There is a broad difference in the Bible between joy and jollity; the one often comes from above, and the other quite too often from beneath. The cheerfulness which God's Word commends is not dependent on outward conditions or circumstances; for some of the most miserable people in our land may be eating their sumptuous dinner today off silver and porcelain in splendid mansions. It is not where we are, but what we are that determines our real happiness. Christian cheerfulness is that sunshiny, happy

1 Proverbs 17:22.
2 Proverbs 15:15.

frame of mind which comes from health of heart; it is the invariable symptom of heart-health.

Such a temper of mind has a most potent influence upon the bodily health. Many a lean dyspeptic who has no appetite for his food, and no refreshing rest in his sleep, is simply dying of worry and peevishness. The acrid humors of the mind have struck through and diseased the digestive organs. The medicine he needs is not from the physician or the pharmacy. A good dose of Divine grace, with a few grains of gratitude for God's mercies, and a frequent bracing walk of benevolence in helping other people, will do more to quicken his appetite and put healthy blood into his weazened frame than all the drugs of the apothecary. Not only is a merry heart a wonderful tonic to the body; it is a clarifier and invigorator of the mind. The mental machinery will work longer and far more smoothly when the oil of cheerfulness lubricates the wheels.

It is worthy of note that many of the giants in the Christian Church have been men of exuberant cheerfulness. Stout old Martin Luther had in him a huge capacity for laughter; he came home from his stormy public conflicts to make merry with his household around his Christmas tree, and to enjoy music and song with his wife Katherina. Lyman Beecher was as indigenous an American product as the hickory or the buckeye tree; like Abraham Lincoln he tasted of the soil. His heart-health was of the most robust character. With work enough for five men on his shoulders, he was ready to go off and spend a whole day with his boys gathering chestnuts—filling the forest with his laughter and glee. At the close of some of his most powerful revival services he came home to prepare for a wholesome night's slumber by a romp with his children, or a few lively airs on his violin. The same sunny-hearted cheerfulness has been the characteristic of Spurgeon, and Phillips Brooks and Newman Hall, and Guthrie, and many other masters in Israel—the swing of whose minds, like the swing of a great wave at sea, threw off jets from its foaming crest.

Let me ask the men of business who read these lines, how many of you manage to lubricate the wearing machinery of life with this oil of cheerful spirit? How many of you come home from the exacting care and tear of your daily calling to make your fireside bright and your household happy? I fear that we who profess a religion of joy and hope are too often so chafed by the frictions, or worried by the cares of life, that we bring but little of the "merry heart" into our homes. I have known some specimens of piety that shone in the prayer meeting, but smoked sadly at the fireside. If you Christian fathers and mothers do not make your homes attractive, and winsome, and cheerful, your children will seek other places of attraction that may be by-roads to perdition! A lively dinner once in a twelvemonth is all very well; but far better is the cheerful heart that is a "continual feast" all the year round. How shall this temper of mind that is both meat and medicine, be secured and maintained? A few simple prescriptions may not be amiss. In the first place, look at your mercies with both eyes, but at your trouble with only one eye. Look at your mercies and your privileges often, and at troubles when you cannot help it. If adversities press heavily, draw all the honey you can out of the hard rock, and oil out of the flinty rock. Saadi, the Persian poet, tells us that he never complained of poverty but once, and that was when he had no money to buy shoes; but meeting a man who had no feet, he became contented to go barefooted. If a heathen could keep cheerful by his philosophy, why should a Christian believer ever complain who is the heir through Christ to a magnificent eternal inheritance?

Strive to reach Paul's secret: "In whatsoever state I am,

I will be content." In these days of extravagance keep down the accursed spirit of grasping. By all means live within your means. You do not need all the coal to heat your little oven. Most of my readers may have as large possessions now as they can give good account of at the Day of Judgment. Godliness with contentment is great wealth. A millionaire once said to me, "I never got any real happiness out of my money until I began to do good with it." Be useful if you want to be cheerful. Always be lighting somebody's torch, and that will shed its lightness on your own pathway, too.

Finally, make a loving God your trustee, and commit your soul to his keeping. Take short views. If you have enough to meet your legitimate wants, and something over for Christ's treasury, don't torment yourself with the fear that your cruse of oil will give out. If your children cluster around your board today, enjoy the music of their voices without racking your hearts with the dread that one may be carried off by the scarlet fever, or another may come to disaster. Faith carries present loads, meets present dangers, feeds on present promises, and commits the future to a loving Heavenly Father. Again I say, take short views. Do not attempt to climb the high wall till you get to it—or fight the battle till it opens—or shed tears over sorrow that may never come. Be careful lest you lose the joys that you have by the sinful fear that God may have trials awaiting you. He promises graces sufficient for today—but not one ounce of strength for tomorrow. You cannot create the morning star; but you can put your soul where Jesus Christ is shining. Each Sabbath is a fitting time to inventory your mercies and blessings. Set all your family to the pitch of the 103RD Psalm; and hang on the wall over your dinner these mottoes: "A merry heart is a good medicine" and "He that is of a cheerful heart hath a continual feast."

Chapter 7

GOD'S LAW OF HELP IN THE FAMILY

Once upon a time two Apostles—Peter and John—went up to the temple at the hour of prayer, and seeing a lame beggar at the "Beautiful Gate" they healed him on the spot. The poor cripple gets a happy restoration; the two Apostles get the ears of the people; and the people, in turn, get the Gospel message which Christ's ambassadors proclaim to them. Peter helps the lame beggar; the restored beggar helps Peter in his Gospel work; both help the assembled multitudes. This illustrates God's appointed law of mutual helpfulness.

One of the designs of our Creator in "setting the solitary in families" is that this law of mutual help might be put into practice. "None of us liveth to himself" might be written on the lintel of every household. At the very outset of our existence, in earliest infancy parental love becomes a real though imperfect miniature of the Divine Providence. The sweet, sacred name "mother" means life, food, medicine, protection and about all things else to the dependent child. In good, patient mother's arms the little mendicant finds its "Gate Beautiful." There is its garner of food, there its soft couch of repose, there its store of cordials for hours of pain, there its playground of infant glee, there its harbor of refuge and stronghold of safety.

God typifies his own tenderness when he says, "as one whom his mother comforteth, so will I comfort you."[1]

Does the receiver of all these parental bounties yield nothing in return? Getting so much, does the little cherub (for the most homely child is a cherub to the mother's eye) give nothing in return? Tell me, ye who have held a budding immortality next to your throbbing bosom, has that little nursling nursed no deep and holy thoughts, no sweet ecstasies, and no unutterable emotions in your own heart? Thou lonely and meek-eyed mother, when through the long weary hours of absence from him who was at his daily toil, or out upon the rocking deep, you grew sad and timid and lonesome, tell me, if you can, what a wealth of companionship you found in two little bright eyes and the music of a merry tongue. How brave you grew when you remembered that you were the guardian angel of that God-given treasure! When you began to teach the earliest lessons to your darling, did you not find that your child was educating you as rapidly as you were educating it? Have you learned no lesson of patience as you bent over the crib where pain was moaning at the midnight hour? Have you been taught no self-control when you saw passionate temper rising in that young breast, and no lesson of unselfish love when you were ready to sacrifice time and ease and rest and strength for that darling's welfare? Ah, there are some mothers who read these lines that have learned what God could nowhere else have taught you, when you swallowed down your tears over that little coffin and hung (as in a strange dream) over that deep, deep grave that seemed to reach down into eternity.

Thank God for children, living or dead, here or in Heaven! A childless home is like a leafless, blossomless tree; the summer winds make scant music through the boughs, and the summer

1 Isaiah 66:13.

sun ripens no fruit on the branches. A cradle is often a "Gate Beautiful" in life where the soul receives some of the most precious gifts of healing; a gate through which the heart often finds its way up to the throne of God and out into the mysteries of the eternal world. Most profitable instructors may our children be to us in many ways. Believe it, O parents, that when God sets a child in the midst of us he puts a looking-glass there to see ourselves in. Our faults or our vices are often made to glare back terribly from the countenance and the conduct of those who sin our sins over again. Sharp schooling that, where the parent becomes the pupil! On the other hand, when I have seen a truly Christian pair looking with grateful joy on the child of their love as he came home with his prize from school, or as he stood up before the church to confess Jesus Christ in the fresh beauty of a youthful self-consecration, then I saw the mirror of childhood giving back the beautiful reflection of parental piety and grace. The early death of children has often been turned to a glorious gain by the conversion of their parents; no trial is so often made a sanctified trial as that. The hand of a departed darling has led father or mother, or both of them, Christward.

It is not only in the relation of parentage and childhood, but also in every other relation, that the family is a school of mutual help. Each member depends on every other. Today the robust father holds the "wee laddie" on his knee, or leads him up the stairway of that schoolroom in which he is to be taught his alphabet. There is a tomorrow coming by and by when the lisper of the A, B, C will be the master of a home of his own, with an infirm, gray-haired parent dozing away his sunset years in an armchair. What a constant benediction is a sunny-faced grandmother in many a house! Her chair is the next most sacred thing to the family altar. God intends that parents and their offsprings shall never issue a "declaration of independence." Each is to help the other when and where help is most needed; and every word and deed of unselfish love comes back in fifty-fold blessings on its author.

A brave girl of my acquaintance is toiling hard not only for self-support but to educate a little brother; and I know a noble eldest son who is carrying all his little orphan brothers and sisters on his sturdy back. The sick members of the household have their useful ministries also. In many a home there is a room whose silent influence is felt all over the dwelling. The other members of the family come in there to inquire after the sick sufferer, to bring fresh flowers or choice fruit, to read aloud to her, or to watch with her through the lonesome night. That room is the "Gate Beautiful" of the house; from it steals forth an influence that makes every one gentler and tenderer and more unselfish.

The home is God's primal training-school. He puts there feeble babes, and sweet invalid daughters, and crippled boys, and infirm grandparents, for this purpose, among others, that the strong may bear the burdens of the weak, and in bearing them may grow stronger themselves in Bible graces. Invalids and children have their uses to help the well-grown and the vigorous as well as to be helped by them. In every Christian family the scene at the Beautiful Gate of Jerusalem's temple is repeated over and over again when the wise and the strong take the weaker by the hand and say, "Rise up; I will help you *walk.*" Underneath the foundations of the commonwealth is the family, and the oldest of all Churches is the "Church of the house." Of that Church the parent is the pastor.

Chapter 8

WHY NOT REJOICE MORE?

Every child of God may well rejoice because he has such a Father in Heaven. "I have set the Lord always before me; therefore my heart is glad, and my glory rejoiceth."[1] In his presence is fullness of joy. This refers to the experiences of the present life, and then up at his right hand will be the "pleasures forever more." It is a bad heart that skulks away from a loving Father in sullen distrust and dread. Then, too, what joy is kindled in our souls when we are brought into full reconciliation with God through the atoning love and meditation of Jesus Christ! The returning prodigal's heart thrills under every kiss of his forgiving Father.

> "Earth has a joy unknown in heaven,
> The new-born peace of sins forgiven.
> Tears of such pure and deep delight,
> Ye angels, never dimmed your sight."[2]

The assurance of a full salvation is enough to keep our

---

1 See Psalm 16:8, 9.
2 A quote from *Forgiveness of Sins a Joy Unknown to Angels* by Augustus Lucas Hillhouse.

hearts aglow. "I give unto you eternal life," says our omnipotent Saviour, "ye shall never perish, neither shall any man
pluck you out of my hand."[1] All things work together for good
if we love God. Even sharp pruning may make us yield richer
clusters of spiritual fruit, if we will let God have his way. And
when the discipline and conflicts of this earthly school-life are
ended, we look upward, and see that "our names are written
in Heaven."

All these joys our loving God provides for us, and offers
them to us. We cannot create canary birds; but we can provide
cages for them, and fill our rooms with their music. Even so
we cannot create the rich gifts which Jesus offers; but they are
ours if we furnish heart-room for them. The birds of peace
and contentment and joy and gratitude will fly in fast enough,
if we will only invite Jesus Christ and set the windows of our
souls open for his coming. Every time that we perform a kind
Christ-like service to the poor, the neglected, or the wronged,
another canary bird flies into our window. The blessedness of
giving is returned with compound interest.

Now with all these pure and substantial joys within our
reach, it is a sin and shame for a genuine Christian to be
wretched. Is not disobedience to God a sin? He commands to
rejoice. No duty is more clear. "Rejoice in the Lord always, and
again I say rejoice![2] The joy of the Lord is your strength."[3] You
can fill your soul with inspiring thoughts, and with memo-
ries of mercies; you can occupy your soul with plans of doing
good to others and with acts of obedience to the inward voice
of Christ, such as will kindle your soul into a glow. A noble
woman of my acquaintance makes rainbows on the cloud of

1 John 10:28.
2 Philippians 4:4.
3 Nehemiah 8:10.

her widowhood by ministrations of mercy to the poor and the destitute. There is a "godly sorrow" over our shortcomings, and over our woes and wrongs of others that every Christian ought to feel; but such sorrow must never be allowed to drown out the deep abounding joy of the Lord down in the very core of our souls. There is a gulf-stream of God-given joy that ought to send its warm current through the wintriest waves of trials and adversities.

All the coal-beds in Pennsylvania and Ohio are only solidified sunshine. The love of Jesus streaming down into your soul makes the central heat; that heat generates spiritual power. So doth the joy of Jesus become your perennial strength. A doubting ague-smitten Christian cannot do much but shake. A back-sliding Christian is on his road to a cell in the castle of Giant Despair. But "he who is nearest to Christ is nearest to the fire," and the contact keeps the heart aglow. Why not rejoice more? Count up your golden mercies, count up your exceeding great and precious promises, count up your joys of heirship to an incorruptible inheritance, and then march on the road heavenward shouting.

Chapter 9

GROWING OLD AND KEEPING YOUNG

Since the time when Cicero wrote his immortal treatise on Old Age, innumerable screeds have been written on this venerable topic; but as it is an experimental matter, there is always room for another one's experience.

Some people regard old age as a disgrace and practice cunning devices to conceal it. Their wigs and other pretences wear out and expose their folly; for Solomon declares that a hoary head is a crown of glory, if it be found in the way of righteousness.

That old age is an incurable malady is only partially true, for some vigorous persons pass fourscore years without ever having caught it; or they have it so lightly that nobody suspects them. "Old" is a relative term after all. I have known people who were rather pitiably old at fifty; and when I met that swift-footed Christian, William E. Dodge (senior), at the age of seventy-five, with the brisk gait of a boy, and with scarcely a gray hair on his head, I said to him, "You are one of the youngest men in New York."

How to keep young—that is the problem; and it is a vitally important problem, for it really means, how to make the most of life, and to bring the largest revenue of service for the Master.

Healthy heredity counts for a great deal. Longevity runs in certain clean-lived families. For example that stalwart philanthropist, Neal Dow, alert at ninety-two, told me that his Quaker father reached ninety-four, his grandfather eighty-five, and his great-grandfather ninety. Such inherited vigor is a capital to start with, and not to be wasted. On the other hand, one of the most atrocious crimes is that committed by some parents, who not only shorten their own days, but make long life an impossibility to their offsprings.

Supposing that a man has a fairly good and unmortgaged constitution to start with, there are several practices and methods to ward off the infirmities of a premature old age.

The first and most important is—to *keep the commandments*. Our Creator has written certain laws on our mortal bodies—laws as irrepealable as those written on the stone tables of Sinai; laws for the breach of which Jesus Christ has made no atonement. To squander vital resources by violating these laws, or even by neglecting them, is an unpardonable sin.

There are suicides in Christian churches—yes, in some Christian pulpits! Rigid care as to a digestible diet does not mean fussiness. It means a clear head, clean blood, and a chance of longevity. Stimulants are dangerous just in proportion as they become indispensable. Hard brain-work, hearty eating, and no physical exercise are the short road to a minister's grave. That famous patriarch of the New England pulpit, Dr. Nathaniel Emmons, who was vigorous at ninety-five, used to say, "I always get up from the table a little hungry." The all-comprehensive rule of diet is very simple—whatever harms more than it helps, *let alone*. Willful dyspepsia is an abomination to the Lord.

A second essential to a healthy longevity is the repair of our resources by sound and sufficient *sleep*. Insomnia is worse than any of the plagues of Egypt; it kills a man or woman by inches. How much sleep is absolutely necessary to bodily vigor must be left to Nature! she will tell you if you don't fool with her. "Burning the midnight oil" commonly means burning up life before your time. Morning is the time for work; one hour before noon is worth five after sunset.

When a man has as much strain on his brain and on his nervous sensibilities as most ministers have goes to his bed-room, he should school himself to the habit of dismissing all thought about outside matters. If he has difficulty in doing this, he should pray for divine help to do it. This suggestion is as applicable to hard-worked business men and to care-laden wives and housekeepers as it is to ministers or brain-workers in any profession.

That wonderful physical and mental phenomenon of this century, Mr. Gladstone, once told me that he had made it a rule to lock every affair of State and every other care outside of his bedroom door. To this excellent habit he attributed his sound sleep, and to his refreshing sleep he largely attributed his vigorous longevity. Paddy's rule is a good one—"When you slape, pay *attintion* to it." Personally, I may remark that it is to a full quota of slumber at night and a brief nap after a noon meal that I owe fifty-six years of steady work without a single Sunday on a sick-bed.

To keep young, every man or woman should endeavor to graduate their labors according to their age. After threescore and ten lighten up the loads. It is *overwork* that wears out life; just as it is the driving of a horse after he is *tired* that hurts him and shortens his days. But while excess of labor is injuri-ous to the old, an entire cessation from all labor is still worse. A workless life is commonly a worthless life. If a minister lays off the burdens of the pastorate, let him keep the tools sharp by a ministry-at-large with pen and tongue. When a merchant or tradesman retires from business for himself, let him serve the public, or aid Christ's cause by enlisting in enterprises of philanthropy.

Rust has been the ruin of many a bright intellect. The celebrated Dr. Archibald Alexander, of the Princeton Theological Seminary, kept young by doing a certain amount of intellectual work every day so that he should not lose his touch. He was as full of sap on the day before his death as he was when a missionary in Virginia at the age of two-and-twenty. He prepared and often used a prayer that was so beautiful that I quote a portion of it for my fellow disciples whose life-clock has struck threescore and ten:

"O most merciful God, cast me not off in the time of old age; forsake me not if my strength faileth. May my hoary head be found in righteousness. Preserve my mind from dotage and imbecility, and my body from protracted disease and excruciating pain. Deliver me from despondency in my declining years, and enable me to bear with patience whatever may be Thy holy will. I humbly ask that my reason may be continued to the last; and that I may be so comforted and supported that I may leave my testimony in favor of the reality of religion and of Thy faithfulness in fulfilling Thy gracious promises. And when my spirit leaves this clay tenement, Lord Jesus, receive it! Send some of the blessed angels to convoy my inexperienced soul to the mansions which Thy love has prepared; and O, may I have an abundant entrance ministered unto me into the Kingdom of our Lord and Saviour Jesus Christ."

This beautiful petition flooded his closing years with sweet peace and a strength unbroken to the last.

A sore temptation to the aged is a tendency to querulousness and pessimism. Losses are unduly lamented, and gains are not duly recognized. While we cherish and cling to many of the things that are old, and are all the better for having been tested, let us not seek to put our eyes in the back of our heads and live only in the past. Keep step with the times; keep sympathy with young hearts; keep in touch with every newborn enterprise of charity, and in line with the marchings of God's providence. A ten minutes of chat or play with a grandchild may freshen you more than an hour spent with an old companion or over an old book.

Above all, keep your hearts in the love of God, and walk in the warm sunshine of Christ's countenance. Our "Indian Summer" ought to be about the most golden period of a life consecrated to Him who bought us with His precious blood.

> Eye hath not seen, tongue hath not told,
>   And ear hath not heard it sung,
> How buoyant and fresh—though it seems to grow old—
>   Is a heart for ever young.[1]

---

1 A quote from *The Song of Seventy* by Martin Tupper.

Chapter 10

TEXTS THAT HAVE HELPED AND COMFORTED ME

oleridge's remark that "the Bible is the only book that always finds me," has been abundantly verified in the experiences of myriads of Christians. Other cisterns of thought run dry; this divine fountain of all truth is inexhaustible. For every mood of mind, for every perplexity, every emergency, and every trial there is a precious message for us. My dear old mother's Bible had its margins lined with pencil marks against her favorite and well-tested texts.

There is one text that has helped me wonderfully; it is that not unfamiliar one in the fifty-fifth Psalm; "Cast thy burden upon the Lord." The Hebrew word translated "burden" signifies that which is given to us to bear. The Psalmist means to say that whatever Providence appoints to us, we must lay it upon the Lord. He has cast thy lot for thee; then cast thy lot upon Him. It may seem at first sight as if there was a contradiction between this text and that other one, "Every man shall bear his own burden." But there is no contradiction at all. We have our duties to perform, sometimes very difficult duties; God does not release us from them, but He sustains us in doing them. The load laid upon us does not crush us, for He gives us strength equal to our day; we lay the load upon the strength which our loving Father imparts to us. God's wonderfully gracious offer to us in this text is to lighten our burdens by putting Himself, as it were, into our souls and underneath the burdens. This is a supernatural process; and the whole walk of faith through life is the simple but sublime reliance upon the almighty arm that is never seen but often felt.

This is a world of worries, and all around us are overloaded people; each one thinks his or her burden is the biggest. In the meantime our merciful Father keeps saying to every one of them, "Cast thy burden upon the Lord, and He shall sustain thee."[1] As if this one offer were not enough it is repeated again in the New Testament: "Cast all your *anxieties* upon Him, for He careth for you."[2] This is the more accurate rendering in the Revised Version; for the word translated "care" in our Common Version does not signify wise forethought but that wretched thing *worry*. This text has been delightfully helpful to me because I have a natural tendency to anxieties, and the reason given for rolling them over upon God is very tender and very touching. "He careth for you." He takes a deep interest in you. He has you on His infinitely loving heart. He is the One who says to me, "My child, don't break yourself down with that burden." The infinite Ruler of the Universe, who is wise in counsel and wonderful in working—the God who guarded the infant Moses in his cradle of rushes; who sent His messenger-birds to Elijah by the brook Cherith; who quieted Daniel among the ravenous lions, and calmed Paul in the raging tempests—He it is who says to us, Roll your anxieties over on me, for I have you on my loving heart! What fools we often are, when we trudge along with bended backs and weary, careworn hearts; and all the while God's omnipotent arm is stretched out to relieve us.

1 Psalm 55:22.

2 1 Peter 5:7.

These twin-texts I have just quoted have more than once exorcised that demon of "worry," and made me move nimbly over the path of duty. Sometimes in a season of great perplexity a passage of Scripture has suddenly darted its light upon me, and made the pathway very clear to my eyes. A remarkable illustration of this occurred to me during my ministry in New York. My field of labor was a very difficult one, and a very attractive call was put into my hands from a prominent, wealthy, and prosperous church in Chicago. The invitation from that church was pressed upon me for several months most persistently. I became sorely perplexed and sought divine guidance. One day I opened that richly suggestive book, "Cecil's Remains," and my eye rested on a passage in which Richard Cecil remarks that changes in life are often dangerous, especially if they appeal to selfish ambition. Then followed this text from the prophet Jeremiah, "Why gaddest thou about to change thy way?" I had never noticed this peculiar passage before, and it decided me in an instant. Never have I ceased to thank God for that little text; but for it I might have missed a distinct call from God to come—soon afterwards—to this city of Brooklyn, in which I have been permitted to do the most important work of my life.

We ministers are constantly required to administer consolations to afflicted souls, and we are often in sore need of heaven-sent comfort ourselves. Once when God had smitten the four corners of my house by the death of a beautiful and beloved daughter, the following text came to me like a dove of peace flying into my window: "And now men see not the bright light which is in the clouds; but the wind passeth and cleanseth (or cleareth) them."[1] A very dark cloud of bereavement was overhanging me. I needed some revealing wind to

1 Job 37:21.

clear away the dark and dreadful mystery of that affliction and let some ray of light into my troubled heart. One of the truths that beamed in upon me was that there is a great want in all of Christ's ministers who have had no personal education in the bearing of sharp trials. I saw that I needed some lessons that could only be learned through tears, just as Paul needed a thorn in the flesh, and Joseph needed to be shut up in a prison in order that he might reach a palace and a premiership in the kingdom of Egypt. I needed to be taught for myself that dark clouds often rain down precious blessings; that Christ's people are never so exalted as when they are brought low, never so enriched as when they are emptied, never so advanced as when they are set back by adversities, and never nearer a crown than when they are under a cross.

If affliction drives us from God it becomes a curse; if it sends us closer to Him it becomes a priceless blessing. Through the parted clouds of sorrow, O, how many angels of mercy descended upon me! One of them said to me, "Whom I love I chasten."[1] Another angel said, "All things work together for good to them that love God."[2] Another said, "Let not your heart be troubled; believe also in me."[3] Still another angel voice whispered, "This affliction, which is but for a moment, shall work out a far more exceeding and eternal weight of glory."[4] And so, as my vision was cleansed with tears I began to see the bright light breaking through the clouds; and that text has been fraught with precious comfort to me ever since.

I might quote many other passages that have rendered infinite help and consolation; but I close with an incident that

1 See Hebrews 12:6.
2 Romans 8:28.
3 John 14:1.
4 See 2 Corinthians 4:17.

happened in my own household very recently. A few weeks ago a beloved member of my family was compelled to undergo a very severe and critical surgical operation in order to save her life. On the morning of the day that the surgeon was to operate, she opened her little book of "Daily Light," and the text for that day at the top of the page was this: "Thou shalt be steadfast, and shalt not fear; because thou shalt forget thy misery and remember it only as waters that pass away."[1] Those words came like a voice from heaven; and they were as cheering as they have since proved to be prophetic. Truly God's book is a wonderful treasure-house of truth for every step in our pathway of life and every emergency that we encounter. Happy is he who makes it a lamp unto his feet, and the song in the house of his pilgrimage.

---

1 Job 11:15, 16.

Chapter 11

GOD'S GOOD GUIDANCE

Luck is a word that ought to be banished from a Christian's vocabulary; for life is not a lottery and this world is not governed by chance. Our Heavenly Father's precious promise is, "I will teach thee in the way which thou shalt go; I will guide thee with mine eye upon thee."[1] When the children of Israel were making their long march from Egypt to Canaan a miraculous pillar of cloud overhung their camp. In the morning, when Israel was to move onward the cloud gathered itself into the upright column, and pioneered the way in which Moses was to march. All that the Israelites had to do was to watch the cloud.

We may sometimes envy those pilgrims of the desert who were only obliged to look out of their tents in order to learn whether they were to remain quiet or go ahead; and if they were to move they knew just whither to bend their steps. But our God, if we ask him, will be as truly with us in our life-journey as he was with the children of Israel. He will be our guide even unto death. We have his infallible Book as a lamp to our feet, and a light upon our pathway; and in dark hours of bereavement what a cheerful gleam it pours into sorrowing

1 Psalm 32:8.

homes and hearts! One of the best proofs that my Bible is God's book is that it has a clear "thus sayeth the Lord" over the path that leads to heaven, and a most distinct "thou shalt *not*" over the enticing gateways that lead downward toward hell. As the night-watchman beside a railway track swings his red lantern in token of danger, so our loving Father holds out what may be called his red lights of warning and prohibition on the pathways to ruin.

Not only does every true believer have his Bible for his rule of faith and practice, but he is promised the instruction and help of the Holy spirit. "He will guide you into all truth."[1] In addition to this, the docile and obedient believer has the example of his Master, who has said, "He that followeth me shall not walk in darkness, but shall have the light of life."[2] There have been some extravagant things said about walking "in *his* steps," but certain it is that if all Christians would examine their Master's footprints they would oftener discover their own path of duty, and would not stray into the seductive roads to self-indulgence, and worldly conformities. "Follow me" means—go where you can have my presence and my blessing; if we cannot carry Christ and a clean conscience with us, then *not one step!*

The infallible Word and the help of the Holy Spirit and the example of our Lord are not all that we have to direct us. There is also what we may call the *pillar of Providence*. We often talk about "special providence" because we can then detect the leadings of God's hand more clearly than at other times; but the whole government of God in regard to us may be a complex series of overseeing and orderings. Sometimes the workings are exceedingly complex; just as in a watch the wheels move in

1 John 16:13.
2 John 8:12.

opposite directions, yet the one mainspring drives them all, and on the dial-plate we read the meaning of the movements. The most vital steps in life turn on small pivots. The Bible abounds in the stories of special providences from Pharaoh's daughter going down to bathe in the Nile to Philip's meeting the eunuch on his way to Gaza. Livingstone intended to go to China; but while he was boarding in London, Robert Moffat happened in one evening, and talked to the boarders about Africa; that talk decided the young Scotchman towards the most wonderful missionary career of the nineteenth century. Nearly every minister may have his experience of the divine guidance. After long and painful perplexities about accepting a certain attractive call, I opened a book and read this seldom noticed text, "Wherefore gaddest thou about to change thy way?"[1] In an instant I made a decision on which the major portion of my whole life-work has turned. My faith forbids me to believe that this incident was a matter of haphazard chance.

One important thing with the children of Israel was to keep their eyes on the movings or the restings of the cloud-pillar. They did not move it; the cloud moved them. A Christian who would be happy and successful in his spiritual life must be an *open-eyed* servant of his Master. He must come to his Bible not to read his own preconceived opinions *into* the Book, but bring God's teachings *out* of the Book. He must be open-eyed to study his Lord's example, "Looking unto Jesus" signifies not only the ground of our salvation, but the guidance of our conduct. We must be open-eyed to our seasons of earnest prayer, to discover what responses our consciences give; for the Holy Spirit often works on a good conscience as the noonday sun does on a sea captain's quadrant. Especially must we keep our eyes clear and "single" to watch the leadings of Providence.

1 See Jeremiah 2:36.

Does the cloud very evidently move? Then pull up tent-pins, and be ready to go where it guides you. Paul was not the only minister who had the divine direction to his right field of labor. Every Christian also—whether pastor, or teacher, or parent, or whatever he or she may be—who longs to win souls must be on the lookout for opportunities. I fear that *lost* opportunities will cast a shadow on the golden pavement of heaven with more than one of us!

Finally, let us watch for the cloud, and walk by the cloud of God's good guidance. Study the Book. Study Christ, and study Providence, and you will seldom make a serious mistake in life. God will show you by the way he leads you whither he desires you to go. The pillar of cloud will only be needed until you and I get to the Jordan. On the other side of the parted river is the flashing glory of the New Jerusalem! March by the cloud till you reach the crown!

Chapter 12

THE RAINBOW ABOUT THE THRONE

 very common source of error is a distorted view of the character of God. Some persons take a very one-sided view of him, and a simple attribute is taken for God himself. For example, there are some who fix their eyes alone on the divine love, and when they preach, they only exhibit a Being of infinite and unmixed compassion. There is no cloud of holy wrath against sin in their azure sky, and no place for a hell in their rose-water theology. A whole class of solemn Bible-truths they consign to the waste-basket.

Another type of theologians, with equally distorted vision, can see only the divine attribute of justice and holy abhorrence of sin. When a man of this type preaches, he makes his hearers listen only to the incessant thunderings of Sinai; and before their eyes he presents only a "certain fearful looking for judgment and fiery indignation." His half-truth becomes serious error; he may awaken sinners, but he does not make Christians. He has a Sinai, but no Calvary.

To neither of these opposite types of theologians does God appear in his true and adorable attributes of infinite perfection. No such distorted view of our heavenly Father was revealed to that solitary dweller on the isle of Patmos when he beheld a great white throne and Him who sat upon it. "He that sat there was to look upon like a jasper and a sardine stone; and there was a *rainbow round about the throne* in sight like unto an emerald."[1] Out of the throne proceeded lightning and thunderings; yet above it hung the soft effulgence of the rainbow. Mysterious as that apocalyptic vision was, it certainly does illustrate the sublime truth that, the infinite Justice of God is overarched by his infinite Mercy that crowneth its terrors as with a robe of glorious light. The glory of these divine attributes is in their perfect harmony. Separated, one would become weakness, and the other would become cruelty; one would fill heaven with unrepentant rebels, and the other would consign every transgressor to a hopeless perdition. When viewed together, we "behold the goodness and the severity of God";[2] combined together, they have given birth to a scheme of Redemption that will be an object of adoring wonder while eternity endures.

The tender mercy of our heavenly Father began with the beginnings of the human race, and runs on down through all history. When our forefather committed that great primal sin of disobedience, the divine mercy rainbowed the cloud of divine displeasure by the promise of a Saviour. When the gates of Eden closed behind him, gates of Gospel mercy began to open before him. Even that physical curse, "in the sweat of thy face shalt thou eat bread until thou return unto the ground,"[3] hath in it the seed of many blessings. Without the toil to earn it, the bread would lose half its relish; without the fatigues of labor, sleep would lose half its sweetness. Verily, the effects of that primal curse have been so disposed that justice has ended

1 Revelation 4:3.
2 Romans 11:22.
3 Genesis 3:19.

in loving kindness, and the sentence pronounced at the gates of Eden has gone out into multiplied blessings.

That sorrow came into this world as the bitter fruit of sin is the common faith of Christendom. Yet sorrow and suffering are not unmixed evils; affliction is often the school in which the noblest characters are formed. How often we misread what may be called permitted providences! It was a terrible trial to the ancient patriarch that his favorite son Joseph was taken from him. "All these things are against me," is the burden of his pitiful wails. While he is wailing, the caravan heaves in sight that brings to him the tidings that Joseph is alive; and he is prime minister of Egypt. What Jacob's wicked sons "meant for evil" God had turned into a blessing. A Hebrew mother once named her boy Jabez, "because I bore him with sorrow." Yet the child that was born in grief and given a sad name grew up to be the ornament of her house, and "more honorable than his brethren." His history was like the April showers, which begin with weeping clouds, and end in brilliant sunbursts, and in rainbows painted on the sky. Good friends, have not you and I often had rich mercies brought to us under a very dark pall? Yes, and some of our richest blessings have come to us when our righteous Father was punishing us for our sins. God chastises us in love; and the difference between a true Christian and a sham Christian is that one mourns over sins, and the other never minds it. Blessed are they that mourn— and *mend!* Compunction of a godly sort tends to growth in grace. There are too many dry-eyed Christians in this world. There ought to be more tears of penitence over neglects of duty to our fellow-creatures, and over violations of Christ's commandments; then they that sow in the tears of contrition would reap in the joys of pardon and increased spiritual power. Those are the tears that make rainbows.

Let us go back now to the point whence we started, and look at the most wondrous way in which the justice of the holy God is overarched by his sovereign mercy—and that is in the glorious scheme of Redemption. In these times I fear that the great central doctrine of the Atonement is not presented as often and as Spiritually as it ought to be. Phillips Brooks was right when he said that "the preachers who have moved and held men have always preached doctrine; no exhortation to a good life that does not put behind it some truth as deep as eternity can seize and hold the conscience." Perhaps one reason why that eternal truth of the Atonement is not oftener preached is that pulpit-teachers do not fix their eyes enough upon the exceeding sinfulness and damnableness of sin against a righteous God. They do not listen to the "thunderings from that throne which is like a jasper and a sardine stone."[1] Jehovah is infinitely holy, and the "deep substrata and base of all his ethical attributes are eternal law and impartial justice." Law is as much obligated to punish transgressors as transgressors are obligated to obey law. If God should wink at sin his throne could not stand a moment.

It is only when we fix our eyes upon the crystalline purity of that throne, and listen to the thunders of the divine justice, that we can understand aright and adore aright that magnificent *Rainbow of Redemption* that Christ's atoning work has thrown round about that throne. Jehovah can be just, and yet the justifier of every sinner that repents and believes on and obeys the crucified Redeemer. The atoning blood of Christ is the central fact in the gospel of grace. If we are justified, it is by faith in Jesus's blood; if we are purified, it is because that blood cleanseth from all sin; if we ever gain admission to the shining ranks in heaven, it is because we have washed our robes and

1 See Revelation 4:3, 7.

made them white in the blood of the Lamb. Paul gloried in pointing the eyes of all sinners to that resplendent rainbow of Redemption; it has been the theme of the Wesleys, Chalmers, the Spurgeons, the Maclarens, the Moodys, and the mightiest ministers of our modern times. The man who cannot get into a holy glow in pointing the sinful and the suffering to that rainbow of atoning love, can never hold thoughtful minds under the spell of the "power from high." Lift your eyes often, brethren, toward the great white throne, and get fresh inspiration from that bow of love that flashes like an emerald!

Chapter 13

SWEETENING THE BITTER THINGS

What a fine series of life lessons for the Christian is presented by the journeyings of the children of Israel from Egypt to the Promised Land! Almost every scene illustrates some practical truth or spiritual experience. For example, the Israelites, soon after leaving the Red Sea, and after a weary march over torrid sands, came upon a fountain in the desert. They rush forward eagerly for a refreshing draught. But, alas! the first taste is a taste of disappointment; for the waters are so bitter that neither man nor beast can drink them! At once the murmuring multitude give to the unpalatable waters the name of "Marah," which signifies the waters of bitterness. There is a still more terrible bitterness of disappointment in their hearts. They forget all about their deliverance from the land of bondage and the waves of the Red Sea, and think only of their present troubles. With a mixture of ingratitude and despair, they crowd about their leader and cry out: "What shall we drink?"

Now, this exciting scene beside the fountain of Marah finds a parallel in many a chapter of our life experience; and we read of such in the lives of others. Abraham Lincoln was keenly disappointed because he did not win a certain office under President Taylor, and afterward that he was not elected to the United States Senate; but then he might have missed the most exalted station that any American has won in this century. Young Frederick W. Robinson was disappointed because he did not get a commission in the British army; but God had a better place for him in the army of Jesus Christ as the most brilliant preacher in the Church of England. In our own humble experience we have had some tastes of the waters of Marah. We had set our hearts on some favorite plan or project. Perhaps we were going on a long-coveted tour, and had made all our arrangements. But the day appointed for our departure finds us on a bed of severe sickness, and the medicines we swallow are not as bitter as the disappointment. Selfishness murmurs and chafes under the trial. But presently we begin to discover that the sick-bed lay right on the direct road toward Canaan. We begin to talk with our hearts, and to think over our past lives. We make a fresh covenant with God that if he will restore us to health we will use it for him, and be more fruitful Christians. We take up one precious promise after another and drop it into the fountain of trial, and lo! the bitter waters begin to taste sweeter to us! Prayer becomes sweeter, and Christ's presence sweeter, and something whispers to us; "After all, is not this better for me than the journey to Europe, or to California? Is it not good for me that I have been shut in here with my Saviour?"

Now, this was just what happened to disappointed and murmuring Israel. The Lord showed to Moses a certain tree, which, when he had cast it into the fountain, the waters were made sweet, and the whole multitude drank of them with delight. We do not read that God created the tree by a miracle; he simply "showed" it to Moses. So our heavenly Father does not create a Bible, or an atonement, or a mercy-seat, or the promises, or supplies of grace, expressly for us. His Spirit opens our eyes to see them, and our hearts to enjoy them. He reveals to us the tree of healing which turns a draught of bitterness into a draught of holy joy. And so it is that

> "Trials make the promise sweet,
>   Trials give new life to prayer;
> Bring us to the Savior's feet,
>   Lay us low, and keep us there."[1]

I do not pretend to be a superior scholar in the school of providence, but many of the best lessons in life have been taught me by disappointment. One lesson we have all learned is that this world was not made and is not managed only for us. If it were, then the sun would shine just when we wanted a fair day, and the rain would fall when our garden needed to be watered. But we have found that God goes right on and orders things as pleaseth him, without consulting us. And when our plans were thwarted, and a little Marah began to bubble up in our hearts, that stern schoolmaster, Disappointment, said to us: "Don't be selfish. This world was not made for you alone. Your loss is another's gain. The rain that spoiled your new mown hay made your neighbor's corn grow; the fall in grain or in dry goods will help yonder poor widow to feed and clothe her children more easily." Wherefore we were reconciled to our losses, and the little Marah began to taste sweeter.

Another lesson taught us by that fountain in the desert is that when we get discontented and rebellious we need a bitter draught to cure us of the wicked habit of murmuring. We learn then to prize the mercies that we had regarded with indifference, and perhaps with ingratitude. Health becomes virtually

1 A quote from *Tis My Happiness Below* by William Cowper.

new mercy to us after a long spell of severe sickness. Even ordinary preaching has a rich flavor to us when we have been shut away from the house of God for many weeks. Spurgeon says that, after a long and wearisome tramp over the Great Aletsch Glacier, in Switzerland, he and his companions became desperately hungry. A peasant went off to obtain some food at a chalet, and came back, bringing some milk that was too sour to drink, and bread that was too black and hard for them to eat. When, after a long pull, they reached their mountain inn, the most ordinary food was inexpressibly delicious. Our thankless hearts often need a Marah of disappointment or privation in order to make us appreciate the good gifts of God for which we cared too little before.

There is not a single person who reads these lines who has not had some bitter cups pressed to his lips. No journey to the heavenly Canaan is trodden without some Marahs on the road. The power and the glory of Christ's grace are in sweetening the draught. I have often sat down beside a child of God who had in her hand a bitter cup of trial, but the sweet breath of Jesus has turned the bitterness into such a blessing that she tastes the love of Jesus in every drop. Grand Old Richard Baxter, after a life of constant suffering, exclaimed: "O, my God, I thank thee for a bodily discipline of eight and fifty years!" That noble and consecrated layman, Harlan Page, of New York, during his last illness uttered these triumphant words: "A bed of pain is a precious place when we have the presence of Christ. God does not send one unnecessary affliction. Lord, I thank thee for suffering. I deserve it; let me not complain or dictate. I commit myself to thee, O Saviour, and to thy infinite love. I stop my mouth and lie low beside thee." So did victorious grace build up that blood redeemed soul faster than disease was pulling down the frail tenement in which it dwelt. And through the rents which coming death was making heaven's glory shone in with a rapturous radiance! These were splendid testimonies. I earnestly hope that in many chambers of sickness, or houses of sorrow, they may be like the boughs from that tree which Moses plucked and cast into Marah, making the waters of bitterness sweet to the thirsty drinkers. God knows best.

> "All the lessons he shall send
> Are the sweetest;
> And his training in the end
> Is completest."[1]

---

1 A quote from *Chosen Lessons* by Francis Ridley Havergal.

Chapter 14

RICH POOR PEOPLE

A letter has just reached me from a venerable lady whose life-clock has reached today the high mark of eighty-eight. She has been for many years the inmate of a charitable "Home" for the aged and the impoverished—a kindly provided "Snug-Harbor" for those whose fortunes have been wrecked by the storms of adversity. This good woman is one of God's heiresses, and is getting part of her great inheritance in this world; for poor as she is in purse, she writes me that she is daily feeding on her Bible, and has just been reading a consolation which has "greatly joyed her heart." No letter of condolence for such a happy soul as that; in God's sight she is one of the richest women in that city. "The Lord is my portion," saith her cheerful soul.

There are plenty of earthly cisterns that are being shattered, or are running dry. The chief thing in the cistern was money, and that has leaked away. The bags that hold a rich man's money are "full of holes." While he is sleeping the fire may consume his warehouses, the gales may wreck his ships, or his stocks and bonds may be dwindling towards worthlessness. I once overtook and walked in a New York street with a man who in former days had been a financial king; I talked with him out of sheer compassion, for he looked so lonesome, and nobody noticed him. His scepter had been broken, and those who had courted him in his days of prosperity had "cut" him in the wintry days of his adversity. His investments had been swept away; and that raises the vitally important question whether there are not some investments in this world that we can make which are absolutely certain never to depreciate?

Yes, there are. The Bible speaks of them as the "portion of the soul." It is an actual solid possession, and it is one that meets the soul's necessities. That man or woman is well off who has what meets and satisfies his or her real wants. Many of the so-called "want" are really fictitious. Daily bread is an actual necessity, and Christ teaches us to pray for that; but a sumptuous dinner is a luxury. It is not really necessary for anyone's health or happiness of heart that he should have a handsome house or a large bank account, or a luxurious table, or high social rank, or any of those things "for which the Gentiles seek." There are certain possessions, however, that are indispensable to our happiness; they are—peace of mind, a clear conscience, the forgiveness of our sins, the favor of God, the chance to be more or less useful, and that infinite wealth that is summed up in having Jesus Christ in our souls.

More than one person who is under the harrow of pecuniary anxiety or some other sharp affliction will read this article, and say, "Well, I wish I could feel as contented as that cheerful old lady in that charity 'Home.' Her fortune had been lost, and yet she is rich; her kindred are gone, and yet she is not lonely." My friend, just inventory the good things that you may have if you will seek for them in the right place and the right way.

The value of a banknote depends on the assets of the bank; and the value of God's promises depends on the resources of His power and boundless love. My friend, just open your casket and read such promises as these: "No good things will He withhold from them that walk uprightly"[1]—"I will never forsake thee"[2]—"My grace shall be sufficient for thee."[3] God never defaults in His promises. Do you crave friendship? Then find a Friend who "sticketh closer than a brother."[4] Are you lonesome? Listen to that sweet voice—"Lo! I am with you always."[5] Are you often distracted with worries? Cast your cares on Him; He careth for you. Just think who it is that says, "My peace I give unto thee."[6] Do you crave a full assurance that all is well with you? Then practice the faith of adherence to Christ. Remember that faith is the milk, and assurance is the cream that rises on it; if your milk is half water, you cannot expect much cream. When income runs down low, invest more in kind deeds to other people; that pays solid comfort. Is your heart aching at the sight of that empty crib, or of that empty chair at your plain table? Then don't let your grief stagnate! it will turn to poison; draw it off by trying to help somebody poorer than yourself. The saddest thing about grief is that it tends to make us brood, and grow selfish. Wealth or poverty, cheerfulness or discontent, sunshine or darkness depends on our own hearts. With Jesus Christ securely there, you are rich. That cheerful letter that inspires this article was written by an aged hand in the "Louise Home" in a certain city. I think the dear Master was whispering to her, as He does to all of us who trust Him—"A little while and ye shall see Me; I go to prepare a place for you, and will come again and receive you unto Myself."[7]

---

1 Psalm 84:11.
2 Hebrews 13:5.
3 2 Corinthians 12:9.
4 Proverbs 18:24.
5 Matthew 28:20.
6 John 14:27.
7 See John 16:16; John 14:2, 3.

Chapter 15

GOD'S KINDNESS TO LAME SOULS

After David had been firmly seated on the throne he inquired whether any of the house of Saul were yet living; for if so, he would like to show them kindness for the sake of his beloved friend Jonathan. An old family steward named Ziba reports to the King that there is a son of Jonathan yet living who is "lame on the feet." This is about the only fact known in regard to the poor waif of a dethroned royal family. He is a cripple. Ever since his nurse had fled from the house at the tidings of Jonathan's bloody death, and dropped the little five-year-old in her panic, he had been incurably lame in both his feet. And so he had been sheltered in the house of one Machir, over on the eastern side of the Jordan.

As soon as David learns that a child of his bosom friend is still in the land of the living, he remembers that he had once made a covenant with Jonathan to show the "kindness of the Lord" to his house forever. He promptly sends one of the royal chariots to Lodebar with orders to bring the poor lame Mephibosheth up to court. When the abashed cripple reaches the palace, and hobbles into the King's presence chamber he is perfectly overwhelmed. He falls on his face, and exclaims, "What is thy servant that thou shouldest look upon such a

dead dog as I am?" Mephibosheth seems to have been a shy
and gentle creature, like many others who suffer from bodily
infirmities; but there is nothing which so soon lays one flat on
the face as a volley of unexpected kindness. No artillery kills
an enemy like a broadside of love. If Mephibosheth had been
taught from his childhood to regard David as the destroyer of
the dynasty of Saul, all his early prejudices must have melted
at once when the monarch received him so graciously. Not
only receives him, but adopts him "for Jonathan's sake" into
the royal household! He sits at the King's board every day and
finds a royal table, "a good hiding place for lame legs." In that
wild age of war, and violence, when revenge was so constantly
practiced, this little cabinet-picture of the fugitive cripple
seated at the imperial banquets has in it the lineaments of the
New Testament Gospel. It is a very pretty parable of God's
mercy to crippled souls.

Every sinner is lamed by sin, and is wholly impotent to
restore himself. When the Holy Spirit awakens a sinner to a
deep conviction of his own guilt, he is ready to confess his
utter unworthiness in language as strong as that used by
Mephibosheth. The godly Rutherford of Scotland describes
himself in the same impassionate language as having once
been a "dead carcass not able to step over a straw." John Bunyan
uses quite as vehement expressions in his "Grace Abounding."
Pungent convictions of personal guilt do not appear to be
as common in these days; but I doubt whether any man
can rightly appreciate the wonderful mercy of God in Jesus
Christ, and the infinite preciousness of atoning love unless he
has been broken down in penitent self-abasement. The lowliest convictions of guilt are usually the prelude to the loftiest
attainments in godliness. The repentant and restored ripples
are those whose feet become "like hinds' feet" in running in

the pathway of God's commandments.

There is a beautiful parallel between David's embassy of kindness to bring up Mephibosheth to Hebron, and the mission of the atoning Saviour to crippled humanity in its far-off wanderings. That royal chariot halting at the poor lame fellow's door to carry him up to the King is a fine figure of divine mercy that stops at the sinner's doorway. Grace furnishes the chariot. Grace sent the only begotten Son of God into the world that whosoever trusteth in Him should not perish but have everlasting life. This home-bringing of the lamed exile to the palace reminds us of that scene where the father welcomes home the wanderer from the far country and kills for him the fatted calf, and clothes him in the goodly robe. This reception of a repentant and believing soul is all for Jesus's sake, even as Mephibosheth was welcomed for Jonathan's sake. Christ's sufferings on the cross and His intercession are at the bottom of every sinner's salvation. When any of us get admission to the marriage-supper in our Father's House, our song will be to Him who came to seek and to save the lost. What a family of restored cripples there will be at that supper of the King!

God's kindness to the lame is not only manifest in the atonement, or in pardon to the penitent sinner or in converting grace; it is shown in His patient forbearance and compassion to stumbling Christians.

For Christians do stumble, and some of them shockingly. Peter was not the first or the last to catch a disgraceful fall; he never would have healed a cripple in the "Gate Beautiful" if his own spiritual lameness had not been cured by his forgiving Saviour a short time before. God's ambulances are kept pretty busy. The difference between an impenitent sinner and a Christian is that the one is willing to continue weak and wicked; the other when he slips and sprains himself is not content to lie on his face, but repents and seeks recovery, and walks more circumspectly. God is very forbearing toward the feeble Christians who like Bunyan's "Ready-to-halt" hobble on crutches; but such slay no giants, reap no harvest, and win no crown. They are not models. When a soul has once been healed by divine grace of its lameness, it ought, like the cured cripple at the temple-gate, to be walking and leaping and praising God.

Chapter 16

THE PARSON'S BARREL

Well, parson," said Deacon Goodgold to his pastor, "that last Sunday morning's sermon was number one prime; may I ask you which end of the barrel that came out on? Your barrel is like the widder's in Scripter; it never seems to give out."

"I am glad that my sermon suited you," replied the genial dominie, "for I got part of that at your house, part came from neighbor B——'s and part from poor Mrs. C——, in whose sick room I spent an hour, and one hint in it came from your boy Frank, who rode by my house on 'old gray' without any saddle or bridle. I picked up some of the best things in that discourse during an afternoon spent in pastoral visiting."

Pastor Honeywell was a shrewd man and a faithful, godly pastor. He had not a great many books, and his family increased faster than his library. His Bible he had at his finger's ends; it was his one great, unexhausted storehouse of heavenly knowledge. But he also had a book of human knowledge second only to God's Word. In the forenoon he studied his Bible, and in the afternoon he sallied out with horse and buggy and studied his people. He rode with his eyes open, finding illustrations—like his divine Master—from the birds of the air, the flowers of the field, and the sower or plowman by the wayside. His mind was on his sermon all the week. If he saw a farmer letting his team "blow" under a roadside tree, he halted and had a chat with him. He observed the farmer's style of thought, gave him a few words of golden counsel, and drove on, leaving the farmer something to think of and something to love his pastor for also. If he saw a boy on his way from school he took the lad into his buggy and asked him some questions which set the youngster to studying his Bible when he got home. Pastor Honeywell caught his congregation when they were young.

Deacon Goodgold was curious to know more about the way in which his minister had gathered up that last Sunday's sermon. "Well," replied the parson, "I was studying on the subject of trusting God in time of trial. First, I went to the fountain head, for my Bible never runs dry. I studied my text thoroughly, comparing Scripture with Scripture. I prayed over it; for a half hour of prayer is worth two hours of study in getting light on the things of God. After I had put my heads and doctrinal points on paper I sallied out to find my practical observations among our congregation. I rode down to your house and your wife told me her difficulties about the doctrine of assurance of faith. From there I went over to your neighbor B——'s house. He is terribly cut down since he failed in business. He told me that, with the breaking down of his son's health and his own breakdown in the store, he could hardly hold his head up, and he had begun to feel awfully rebellious towards his heavenly Father. I gave him a word or two of cheer and noted down just what his difficulties were. From his store I went to see poor Mrs. C——, who is dying slowly of consumption. She showed me a favorite flower that she had put into her window-sill to catch the sunshine, and said that her flower had been a daily sermon to her about keeping her soul in the sunshine of her Saviour's countenance. Her talk braced me up and gave me a good hint. Then I called on the Widow M——, who always needs a word of sympathy. Before I came away she told me that her daughter Mary could not exactly understand what it was to trust Christ and was finding no peace, although she had been under deep conviction of sin for several weeks. I had her daughter called in and I drew from her all the points of difficulty; I read to her such texts of Scripture as applied to her case, prayed with her, and then started home. Your boy rode by my house on the old horse, which went along without any bridle, and stopped when he got to the bars that lead to the pasture.

"Before I went to bed I worked in all the material that I had gathered during the afternoon; and I studied out the difficulties of your wife and of your neighbor B——, and of the troubled daughter of Widow M——, and I wove the answers to such doubts and difficulties in my sermon. The cheerful experiences of good Mrs. C—— in her sick chamber helped me mightily, for faith in action is worth several pounds of it in theory. I went to my pulpit last Sunday pretty sure that my sermon would help three or four persons there, and if it would fit their cases I judged that it would fit thirty or forty more cases. Human nature is pretty much alike, and sometimes when I preach a discourse that comes home close to my own heart's wants, I take it for granted that it will come to plenty of other hearts in the congregation."

"Yes, parson," said the deacon, "your sermons cut a pretty broad swath. I often feel 'thou art the man' when you hit some of my besettin' sins. I have often been wantin' to ask why your sermon barrel has never giv' out, as poor Parson Scanty's barrel did before you came here. He always giv' us about the same sermon, and as I set away back by the door, it got to be mighty thin by the time it got to my pew."

Parson Honeywell turned pleasantly to the deacon and said: "I will tell you what the famous old Dr. Bellamy once said to a young minister who asked him how he should always have material for his sermons. The shrewd old doctor said: 'Young man, fill up the cask, fill up the cask, and then if you want to tap it anywhere, you will get a full stream; but if you put in very little, it will dribble, dribble and you may tap and tap and get precious little after all.' I always get my people to help me fill up the cask. Good afternoon, deacon."

Chapter 17

THE JOYS OF A PASTOR'S LIFE

I t is a lamentable and portentous fact that the number of candidates for the Gospel ministry is steadily decreasing. In one of the leading Protestant denominations they have decreased from 1,508 to 917 within the last five years! At quite a recent graduation of a class of over 200 from one of our greatest universities, about fifty declared their purpose to enter upon commercial business, about the same number were looking to the legal profession, others to the medical and scientific pursuits; but out of all the Christian students in that class only eleven announced their intention to become ministers!

Various reasons may be assigned for this sad falling off of candidates for the pulpit. These I will not discuss; nor would I minimize the difficulties which a faithful, earnest, evangelical minister has to encounter. Some of these difficulties are arguments for multiplying rather than diminishing the number of the right kind of gospel preachers. My purpose is to present the golden side of the shield, and to tell young men of brains and culture and heart-piety what solid and substantial joys they forego when they turn away from a calling that an angel might covet. I do not underrate the need or the usefulness of godly laymen; but there are peculiar satisfactions and honors and spiritual rewards to be won by the preacher who preaches God's glorious messages to men, and the pastor who gathers and feeds and leads the Master's flock.

In the first place, he is in a close and covetable partnership with the Lord Jesus Christ. His work is on the same lines with him who came to reveal the mind of God to sinning and suffering humanity, and to "seek and to save the lost." Christ's great commission to the band of men who were in the most intimate relations to himself was, "As ye go, preach!" They were to be his witnesses, his representatives, his heralds and his ambassadors; and that is the very same commission given today to every man whom he calls into his ministry. If you ask me, "What is a call to the ministry?" I would answer that it is both the ability and the intense desire, with God's help, to preach the Gospel of salvation in such a way that people will listen to you.

In addition to the joy and honor of a peculiar partnership with the incarnate Son of God, every true minister is, in the best sense of the word, a successor of the apostles. Although without their infallible inspiration and miraculous gifts, yet, like them, the faithful minister is the ambassador of the Lord Jesus. The greatest of the apostles, in addressing his spiritual children at Thessalonica, exclaims, "What is our hope or joy or crown of rejoicing? Are not even ye in the presence of our Lord Jesus Christ at his coming? For ye are our glory and joy."[1] Rising above his poverty, his homelessness and his persecutions, the old hero reaches out and grasps his royal diadem. It is a crown blazing with stars—every star an immortal soul plucked from the darkness of sin into the light and liberty of a child of God and an heir of heaven! Poor, he is making

1 1 Thessalonians 2:19, 20.

many rich; he would not change place with Caesar. My young brother, when you are frightened away by foolish fears, or drawn away by worldly ambitions from the Gospel ministry, have you ever thought what an apostolic companionship you are despising? Have you thought of what a joy and crown of rejoicing you are flinging away?

Think, too, of the glorious themes and the sublime studies that will occupy your mind as a minister of God's Word. Is human science elevating? How much more is the science of Almighty God and of man's redemption, and of the unseen realities of eternity? Your themes of constant study will be the themes that inspired the mighty Luthers and Wesleys and Pascals and Chalmers; you will be nurturing your soul amid those pages where John Milton fed, and amid the scenes that taught Bunyan his matchless allegory, and Jeremy Taylor his hearse-like melodies. Every nugget of fresh truth you discover will make you happier than one who has found golden spoil. The study in which a devout pastor prays, and pores over God's Word, becomes an ante-chamber of the King, and he hears the cheering voice of the infinite Love, "I am with you alway."

If the high range of his studies and the preparation of his discourses are so stimulating to an earnest, soul-winning pastor, he finds even richer satisfaction in his pulpit, and in his labors among his flock and the surrounding community. John Bunyan voiced the feeling of such pastors when he said, "I have counted as if I had goodly buildings in the places where my spiritual children were born. My heart has been so wrapt up in this excellent work that I accounted myself more honored of God than if he had made me emperor of all the world or the lord of all the glory of the earth without it. He that converteth a sinner from the error of his ways doth save a soul from death, and they that be wise shall shine as the brightness of the firmament." The young man who enters the ministry with this hunger for souls has "meat to eat that the world knows not of." His purse may be scanty, his parish may be obscure; difficulties and hard work may often bring him to his knees; but while his Master owns his toils with blessings, he would not change places with a Rothschild or an Astor. Every attentive auditor is a delight; and when a returning and repentant soul is led by him to the Saviour, there is not only joy in heaven, but a joy in his own heart too deep for words. It is full measure, pressed down, running over.

Converted souls are jewels in the caskets of faithful pastors; they will flash in the diadem which the righteous Judge will give them in that great day. Even here in this world, it is far better "pay" than any salary for a pastor to be told, "that sermon of yours helped me," or "that one brought me to Christ." During my fifty-six years' ministry I have had an immense correspondence; but the letters that I embalm in lavender are those which express gratitude for a soul-converting sermon, or for words of uplifting consolation spoken either in the pulpit or elsewhere. Happy the minister who is thus helped while he is helping others! He gets a small installment of heaven in advance.

Far be it from me to pronounce the ministry a bed of roses or a hammock of luxury. A faithful, courageous pastor has trials, and not a few temptations; they often attest his fidelity, they sinew his faith and drive him closer to Christ. A whining minister is a disgrace to his calling and an abomination to the Lord. The man who finds that he has mistaken his calling ought to demit the ministry at once. If the ministry were "weeded" tomorrow it would be the stronger.

I do not assert that every able and godly young man in our schools and colleges should enter a pulpit. There are many who can serve their Master and their country more effectively in some other sphere. It is equally true that the only occupation that is not overdone in America is the occupation of serving Christ and saving souls. The only profession that is not overcrowded is the "guild" of good, clear-headed, conscientious, industrious, Christ-loving ministers. Not one such is likely to go begging for a place. They are in demand.

If there may be some in the pulpit who ought to be out of it, there are many out of it who ought to have gone into it. This decrease of candidates for the pulpit is a bad symptom; it shows that the thermometer is falling in the churches. It shows that ambition for money-making and worldly honors is sluicing the heart of God's church and drawing much of its best talent into these greedy outlets. Unless this depletion of the ministry is checked, a woe will be pronounced upon the churches, and a gospel famine will be the penalty. My purpose in this plain article is to send a hailing word of good cheer to the thousands of faithful shepherds of Christ's flocks. It is also to bring before Christian young men in our schools and colleges these two questions: Have I the necessary gifts—mental, physical, and spiritual—for the gospel ministry? If so, can I afford to rob my Master of the service and myself of its joys?

Chapter 18

BRIGHT CHRISTIANS

The houses of the people of Palestine, in ancient times, were not lighted by candles; therefore the translation of the fifteenth verse of the fifth chapter of Matthew in our common version is not correct. In the house of the poorest peasant was a lamp. A small cup or other vessel was filled with oil, a bit of linen rag or a wick was set afloat in it, and the simple contrivance was set on a lamp-stand. To put it under a couch or to hide it under a grain-measure would be absurd. Our Lord, in his sermon on the mount, alludes to the familiar lamp in every dwelling, and then says to his followers *"so* let your light shine before men."[1] This is the manner in which every Christian should be luminous. The word "so" refers back to the previous verse. The motive for doing this then follows, viz., "that men may see your good works, and glorify your Father which is in Heaven." Not for mere ostentation and self-glorification were they to make a display of their religion; neither were they to conceal it by either indolence or cowardice. To turn the outside of their character in would be as harmful as to turn the inside of it out.

The crying want of the times is more *bright Christians.*

1 Matthew 5:16.

There are quite too many church members whose lamps were kindled for a little while—perhaps during the heat of a revival season—and then they have either been smuggled into a dark lantern, or else allowed to die down into a feeble glimmer, barely visible through the smoke. For no mere selfish purpose does Jesus Christ bestow his converting grace upon any man or woman. He did not make you a Christian, my friend, either for your own enjoyment in this world, or to save you from perdition in the next. He touched your heart with his illuminating grace, chiefly that you might impart the benefit of your light to others, and glorify him. He commanded the light to shine into the darkness of your sinful soul, that you might *give* the light of the knowledge of God as seen in the face of Jesus to all with whom you come in contact. You may not be a magnificent Fresnel-burner like a Chalmers or a Wesley in their day, or like a Spurgeon or a Shaftesbury or a Moody in our times. But the properties of light are the same in a household lamp that they are in the huge luminary that flashes from the tower at Sandy Hook; and in your little circle there is just as much need of a bright Christian as there is in the most conspicuous pulpit of Christendom.

If you neglect to let your light shine, however humble it be, not only will your own character suffer, but somebody else will be the worse for it. The simple failure of a signalman to swing his lantern at the right time, has sent a railway train into deadly ruin. Your failure to utter the right word, to do the right thing, or to exert the right influence may be sending some others off the track in the same fatal fashion. I know of certain households—perhaps yours may be one—in which the lamp smokes more than it shines. That son would not be so troubled with skepticism if he saw more attractive living evidence of Christianity in the daily conduct of his professedly

Christian parents. Another son would not be seen so often on his way to the saloon, or some other dangerous haunt, if the torch of both warning and example were held up faithfully and lovingly. It is almost hopeless to expect conversions in some families. One reason is that there is a lamp of profession there which smokes foully instead of beaming brightly. The light that is in that house is fast becoming darkness. The oil has given out. Love of the world, or the greed of selfishness, or some other sin, has extinguished the love of Christ. The real cause of all spiritual declension is the lack of a Christly love and loyalty in the heart. When people are full of any subject they will speak out; they cannot help it. When your soul is on fire with the love of Jesus and of your fellowmen, you will burn and shine unconsciously. Probably the most effective good which most genuine Christians do is in the way of steady, silent, and unconscious reflection of Jesus Christ in their daily conduct. To preach a sermon, or teach a mission-school class, or distribute Bibles or bread among the needy, is a direct, premeditated act of lamp-bearing. But to live along day after day luminously reflecting Christ in word or deed, at home, in the store, in the shop, and everywhere else, is just "*letting* the light shine" of its own accord. That is the sort or religion that tells. And, however glibly Brother A may speak in the prayer-meeting, or however brightly Sister B may shine in her Dorcas Society or "holiness meeting," yet if they end in smoke at home, theirs is but a dark and dreary dwelling. Trim the household lamp, good friends. A revival of thorough *home piety* is the most needed revival in these times, for the well-being of both church and commonwealth.

Light is a combination of many rays, and each white ray a combination of many colors. If you apply the spectrum to a bright Christian, you will find that he sheds out various graces.

Chiefest of all is the ray of *love*. This is the supreme grace which most completely reflects Christ Jesus, and which imparts the golden effulgence to a true, fervent, Christian life. It is not a flash of sentiment, or fitful gush of emotion, but a steady anthracite flame which glows all day and all night because the divine fire is burning in the soul. "So have I loved you," saith the Master; "continue ye in my love." Where this lamp beams, the humblest home will be brightened, the hardest pillow will be softened, the coarsest fare will be sweetened. Love is the best grace Christ can give us, for in it he gives himself; it is the best we can return to him, for in it we give ourselves. . . .

Here are a few of the rays which a bright Christian will reflect, while he is reflecting Christ. Trim your lamp, brother. Feed it afresh with prayer for more oil and with fresh inlettings of Jesus into your soul. Carry your lamp always with you, as the miners carry theirs on their hats, not only to work by, but to help their neighbors work. The world may discover Jesus Christ in you when they would find him in no other way. Light other people's lamps. A bright Christian is a ray shot from the throne of Heaven into this dark world. "Let your loins be girded about, and your lights burning."[1]

---

1 Luke 12:35.

Chapter 19

HOW TO BE CONTENTED

If we can not bring our means to our minds, then let us try to bring our minds to our means." That is an old Puritan minister's version of Paul's cheerful message to his Philippian brethren: "I have learned, in whatsoever state I am, therein to be content."[1] The great apostle was not content to be in a low spiritual state, and therefore he pressed toward the goal of a higher spiritual life every day. But he was content to be where his Master put him, to bear all the hard knocks and endure all the rough usage that he had to encounter in the path of duty. Paul's spirit was like a watch. You may carry it up and down with you, and shake it hither and thither; but the mainspring is not put out of order, nor do the wheels lose their regular motion. Paul was knocked about with cruel treatment and fierce persecutions; but the mainspring of love for Jesus was not broken in his heart, and the wheels of his consecrated activity was undisturbed.

Christian contentment is the cheerful acquiescence of the soul to the will of God in all conditions and under all weathers. It is the habit of the mind, just as faith is the habit of a healthy Christian, and benevolence is the habit of a philanthropist.

---

1 Philippians 4:11.

Like faith it grows by practice, and, like faith, it is learned from God's Word, and is matured by experience. The great, brave apostle learned it where he learned Christ, and he learned it from Christ, and in a pretty severe and costly school. Like every precious thing, we must pay the price for it. And, like most precious things, it is quite too rare, and the thoroughly contented people are in the minority. It is not every young minister who is satisfied to preach Jesus to a hundred new settlers in a frontier log church, or to a few hundreds of poor children in the mission-school of the slums; yet, unless he is willing to be right there and to do just that thing, his Master will sooner put him down lower than say, "Come up higher." We may overrate this grace, but it seems to us that genuine contentment, that is ready to let God have his own way, to let God put us where he chooses, even though the furnace be hot, is more scarce than it ought to be. He or she has attained to it who has learned to say, under disappointments the most bitter, and under trials which give the last turn to the screw and make the blood start, "Thy will, O God, be done!"

This style of contentment is not reserved for sublime occasions; it is visible in all the little, unnumbered events of every-day life. It is patient, not only under death strokes, but under petty vexations and wounding words and neglects; it does not worry over hard seats or boring visitors or stupid servants or a crying child. It manages to be happy in a small house when it can not afford a three-story mansion. So rich is it in God's promises and the sweet smiles of the Master and a good title to heaven, that it does not mind wearing a coarse coat and to trudge on foot toward the better country. It wears the herb called "heart's-ease" in its bosom; it finds a cool spring to drink of in the lowliest vales of life, and catches grand outlooks from the summit of every steep hill it climbs. As it treads along its patient path it chants John Bunyan's quaint, simple song:

> "I am content with what I have,
>   Be it little or much;
> And, Lord, contentment still I crave
>   Because thou blessest such;
> Fullness to me a burthen is,
>   As I go on pilgrimage.
> Here little, and hereafter bliss,
>   Is best from age to age."

Would to God we were all more contented with our mercies and more discontented with ourselves! It is the trying to live on external conditions that makes a Christian restless and wretched. A soul at peace with God and itself, a soul that delights in making other people happy, can sleep sweetly, like the old-time patriarch, with a stone for a pillow.

Chapter 20

JESUS CHRIST THE HEART'S GUEST

The advent of Jesus into a heart that is darkened by trouble is a wonderful source of joy. There is an "upper room" of the soul, an inner sanctum, of which we give up the key only to our nearest and dearest friends. It is inside of that "court of the Gentiles" which all our ordinary acquaintances are treading every day. That inner chamber sometimes becomes what the room in Jerusalem was, on that night after the Master's crucifixion—a place of sore sorrow. A bereaved and forlorn company indeed were the eleven disciples on that evening!

And we feel somewhat as they did. But into our soul's private chamber—when the lights were burning low and the air is heavy with grief or disappointment—there is ONE who enters! He comes in through the closed doors, and O, how sweetly sounds the voice of His love, as He says, "peace be unto you!" He shows us His hands pierced, and His side riven with the cruel spear for our sakes on His cross. When we recognize our divine guest, we are ready to say, in the language of Ray Palmer's sweetest hymn,

"Earth has ne'er so dear a spot
As where we meet with Thee."

At such times of communion with Jesus, we do not need to give to Him the honeycomb; He gives it unto us. Its effusive sweetness makes our lips to sing for joy. His consolations fill the room with their choice perfume. Then we can exultingly say "My beloved is mine and I am His; His left hand is under my head, and His right hand doth embrace me."[1] He spreads the banner of His love over us; we enter into a fellowship of His sufferings for us, and He with our griefs or disappointments. There is no sweeter, stronger fellowship with Jesus than to unfold all our troubles to Him. He lifts off the load. Instead of the spirit of heaviness He giveth the garment of praise. Then like the disciples in the Jerusalem chamber "we are glad when we see our Lord."

It was in anticipation of all the seasons of trial and perplexity and bereavement that should come upon His followers that our Lord gave this precious assurance, "Ye now have sorrow, but I *will see you again*, and your heart shall rejoice, and your joy no man taketh from you."[2] This joy—let us remember—flows from the actual spiritual presence of the Master with us. Peace comes when He comes and power comes also. We become strong with His strength and feel a fresh vigor steal over our fainting spirit. Dark hours bring no fears, for Christ's voice is heard continually saying unto us, "It is I; be not afraid."

To a true believer who is in this close heart-fellowship with Jesus, the largest fortune can add very little; and the loss of earthly property can take but little away. Nothing can break down a soul that is firmly established in this conscious experience. It is united to Him; it is under His wing, and all the clouds that overcast the sky of poor worldlings sail far below it. The hailstorm of trials, adversities and assaults, under which

---

1 Song of Solomon 2:6, 16.
2 John 16:22.

evil men are cowed, cannot hail upward, or reach the believer in his safe place of refuge. His joy is above the reach of the thunderbolts. So Christ Jesus entering into Paul's soul kept him serene amid the Euroclydon tempest—and made Peter to sing in the midnight dungeon; Patmos was no longer a lonely spot to the Beloved Disciple when the Master was with him there.

The more we have of Christ's presence, the more serenely and securely happy we are. An empty heart is a wretched heart. A worldling's treasures never satisfy; the more fuel that is heaped on the fire of covetousness the fiercer is the flame. I don't believe that Rothschild's millions can ever impart such exquisite joy as the saving of a soul gives to many a hard-toiling pastor or Sunday-school teacher. The millionaire will count up his possessions at last and say, "Is this all?" The true Christian inventories his treasures and says "All things are mine and I am Christ's and Christ is God's." A believer's true joy is love clasping Jesus, and faith looking forward to the endless fellowship of heaven. "A little while and ye shall see me; and where I am ye shall be also."

If we make Jesus the guest of our hearts in this world, He will admit us to be His guest in the celestial mansion. When we return home from a long journey, it is not the house, the furniture or the fireside that gives us joy; it is the sight of the loved ones there. So in our Father's House it will not be the pearl-gates or the golden streets—we shall be glad when we see our Lord! In the language of Bonar's sweet hymn—which I heard sung at his funeral—

> Christ will be the living splendor,
> Christ the sunlight mild and tender,
> Praises to the Lamb we render,

    Ah, 'tis heaven at last!

Broken death's dread bands that bound us,
Life and victory around us,
Christ the King himself hath crowned us,
    Ah, 'tis heaven at last!

Chapter 21

SACRED MONEY

In looking over the papers of my beloved and departed mother—who died at the age of eighty-five—I discovered the account-book which contained the expenses of my early boyhood. If it requires financial ability to manage a large estate, it requires still more to eke out a scanty income and make both ends meet. In the list of frugal expenditures made by that widowed mother for an only boy there stood recorded on almost every page the words, "Sacred money." This was sometimes bestowed in making him a life member of the American Tract Society, or the Home Missionary Society, or some other Christian organization. There was also a stout, large envelope which bore the same label, "Sacred money." Into that envelope the good woman was wont to put a certain portion of her very limited income as soon as it came into her hands. When the money was once placed in that wallet the Lord was sure to get His own. Come what might, no demand of luxury or of necessity was allowed to "rob God" of what had been consecrated to His service.

My only apology for this peep of the public eye into a bit of private history is that it reveals the only sure and successful method of practicing systematic beneficence. It fulfils the apostolic rule of "laying by in store" a fixed sum for Christian charity, and then gives conscience the key. To touch a dime of that money for any mere secular use would have been in that godly matron's eyes as egregious a theft as the picking of a neighbor's pocket. That lesson in systematic beneficence has lasted me all my life, and I most earnestly commend it to every Christian parent. Every child should be reared with the firm persuasion that if he gives his heart to Christ, he at the same time gives to Him not only his influence, but a certain reasonable share of his substance. If God's day is held sacred, and God's house is sacred, so should the money that fairly belongs to Him be held sacred likewise. There is no haphazard about this method. The money thus put away and labelled is to be out of the reach of selfishness, and religiously parcelled off for the various objects of benevolence as good judgment directs.

If this system were adopted and practiced in every Christian family, what a revolution it would work! Giving would be regarded as an act of divine worship; the money thus consecrated in advance would be an element in the Sabbath service, and the pastor might fittingly (as some pastors now do) come down from his pulpit and invoke a special blessing on the offerings thus presented cheerfully to the Lord. This system thoroughly carried out would make the contributions of each church not a widely fluctuating, but a fixed and reliable sum from year to year. The great institutions of benevolence could fairly determine their outlay, because they would know their probable income. The curse and stigma of debt would be avoided. The secretaries and directors of our Christian schemes would no longer be kept awake at night by the terrible spectre of "deficiency." The Lord would get His own and the Church would get the blessing, if in every Christian house there was a box or a receptacle that bore the inscription "Sacred money."

In many families the sum thus consecrated might be very small. But gifts to the Lord are to be weighed rather than counted. The two mites of the "poor widow" outweighed the shekels of gold or silver cast by jewelled fingers into the Lord's treasury. The drops make the rivulets, and the rivulets fill the broad lakes. Nine-tenths of all the money that drives the financial machinery of Christ's Church comes from humble stewards, whose "sacred money" is reckoned by dollars and not by hundreds or thousands.

Sometimes small donations yield large results. This reminds me of a pretty incident that I may venture to relate, since it is not likely to meet the eye of the person referred to. When my Brooklyn church, in the days of its infancy, were building their present sanctuary they ran ashore for funds. The Civil War had just broken out, and almost every new church enterprise came to a standstill. On a certain Sabbath I made a fervent appeal for help, and a visitor from New York heard the appeal and went home and spoke of it at his boarding-house table. At the table was a bright young lady who taught in a school and sustained her widowed mother out of her small salary. I had once rendered the young lady some trifling service, which I had quite forgotten, but she had not. The next day she came over to Brooklyn and told me how badly she felt that my church was in such straits. She was not a Christian and had never given anything to any religious object, but she felt desirous to contribute "her mite," and slipped into my hand a bit of paper containing some coin, which I put into my pocket with a word of sincere thanks. After she had gone I opened the paper and found that it contained a fifty-dollar California gold-piece! I immediately sent her word that she must take it back, for I knew that she could not afford to give such a sum. But she wrote me that this, her first gift, had already afforded her such delight she would never allow it to be returned. The next Sabbath I told the story of the gold-piece, and it fired the congregation with fresh enthusiasm and brought in such contributions of funds as tided us over into deeper waters. The young lady herself determined to follow up her gift by coming over to our chapel every Sabbath, and was soon converted, and became a happy member of Christ's flock.

The orphan girl married a young man of fine promise, and they are prominent members of a church in C———. Their two children are winning high honors at college. Verily that orphan girl's gold-piece was "sacred money," and it yielded a grand "dividend." I have told the story of that coin in more than one place where money was being raised under difficulties, and I should not wonder if it were to go on and accumulate still more at compound interest. The Lord's treasury is a wonderful institution; it makes mites turn to millions, it pays magnificent dividends in this world, and its "sacred money" becomes precious treasure in heaven.

Chapter 22

TREASURES IN HEAVEN

"Store away stores for yourselves in heaven." That is the rendering—in one of the earlier English translations of the Bible—of our Lord's injunction in His Sermon on the Mount. He had just told His hearers that the treasures laid up on earth were liable to be consumed by the moth and the rust, or stolen away by thieves. If they wanted to put what was dearest to their hearts out of the reach of the rust and the robbers, they must lodge them in God's keeping; there they would be safe. The shrewdest business man may often lie awake in uneasiness about the absolute security of his investments; the Master declares that what we invest in heavenly treasures can never be lost.

Did Christ mean to recommend a large bestowment of money for charitable purposes in order to secure a place in heaven? Some have twisted this passage into a selfish direction and insisted that almsgiving in this world would purchase salvation in the next world. But our Lord never descended to such a mercenary morality; God is not to be bargained with for gold or silver. The scope of this divine injunction is infinitely wider, higher and holier than any pecuniary transaction for selfish purposes; it has an intensely spiritual significance.

The treasures to which he refers are all those objects for which an immortal being ought to live, and the possession of which are the most pleasing in the sight of God. When any man gives his heart to God, and sincerely aims to give his life to the service of God, he then makes God his trustee. His property may vanish in the flames, or be swept away by commercial hurricanes, but what is dearest to him is secure. "I know whom I have trusted, and I am persuaded that he is able to keep that which I have committed unto him against that day."[1] This precious passage covers more than the salvation of a believer's soul. It embraces all the results and the fruits, and the outcome of a genuine Christian life. The moment that you are truly converted, that moment you begin to make spiritual investments, you begin to lay up heavenly treasures.

The servants of Christ have a different arithmetic from the worldling. He counts his gains by the earthly possessions that he accumulates. The Christian often gains by the losses of earthly things. "He that loses for my sake finds," is an assurance full of good cheer to many a tried and afflicted child of God. Grasping after earthly wealth or honor costs very often a sad loss of grace and godliness. It is not what we take up, but what we are ready to give up, that makes us spiritually rich. Giving up for the sake of our Master honors him, and adds to our treasures in heaven. Therein is the peculiar glory of the martyrs; they counted not even their lives as dear, so that they might honor their crucified Lord, and glorious will be their reward among the crowned conquerors up yonder.

It is impossible to compute what treasures every faithful Christian may be storing away for that celestial storehouse. There is a constant accumulation. There is a "laying up" day by day. God is a just accountant and a generous rewarder.

1 2 Timothy 1:12.

A "book of remembrance" is kept, and God will give to every one as his work shall be. That record on high will read very differently from the assessor's tax-books in this world. Plutus and Midas are assessed in New York or London as millionaires. Up yonder a "certain poor widow" will outshine many of these colossal money-mongers because she put into the Lord's treasury the two mites that were all her living. That box of alabaster which Mary broke over the feet of her beloved Master will not lose its fragrance in heaven. Every act of self-denial for Christ is an investment for heaven. Every word spoken for him here will echo there. A precious encouragement is this for faithful parents and Sunday-school teachers and city missionaries and the whole army of hard toilers in the service of the best of Masters. Do you sometimes get discouraged, my brother, because you do not see more immediate results of your efforts? Don't worry. You are responsible for doing your whole duty; God is responsible for results. His "reward is with him" to give to every servant according as his work shall be.

It goes without saying that, as they who turn many to righteousness will shine as stars in that celestial firmament, there are some favored servants of Jesus who will come into magnificent inheritances in heaven. We can imagine Robert Raikes surrounded by a multitude of those who were the spiritual trophies of his Sunday-schools, and Spurgeon welcomed by the happy souls whom he led to Jesus, and our own Moody finding his heaven all the more joyous for the number of those whom his untiring labors won to the life everlasting. Consecrated talents will then blaze as crowns of rejoicing. What an inducement is this to every young man and woman who is raising the questions: How shall I employ my brains, my culture or my money to the best advantage? Even one talent, if not hidden or wasted, shall make some very humble Christians rich and radiant when they come into their heavenly inheritance.

In these days, and especially in our own country, there is an astonishing increase of men of immense wealth; the word "million" is almost as common as the word "thousands" was in the days of my childhood. Haste to be rich is the prevailing mania; yet only a very, very small proportion of all the most eager seekers after wealth will ever attain it. But every one of my readers may become "rich toward God." The secret of it is to get by giving. This is the true paradox in the economy of grace. He that refuses to give his whole heart to Christ is doomed to perish without Christ. He that saves for self only loses; he that loses for Christ's sake is sure to save. Would you secure treasures in heaven? Then learn to give, and give bountifully. God loveth the cheerful giver. This is not to be limited to gifts of the purse; for the offerings of silver and gold are only a part of what our Master has a right to; we must freely give of everything that we have freely received.

If you have the heart to pray, give your prayers; answered prayers will be part of your heavenly inheritance. You that have acquired wisdom and experience, give your counsels to those who need them. Give your personal labors for Christ and the salvation of souls; no wealthy Christian ought to compound with his Master by drawing a bank check in lieu of personal Christian work. Those who have not much money or counsel, or Christian work to bestow, can afford the blessing of godly living and a holy example. And so a Christly life may be a constant expenditure; even as the noonday sun overflows his golden urn of radiance, and is none the poorer in warmth and brightness.

Such a life is a constant accumulation of heavenly treasures. It is a laying-out here for Christ, and a laying-up yonder. Every good deed is recorded; every victory over sin has its crown; every service for our Lord is remembered; for he hath said, "The reward is with me to give to every one as his work shall be."[1] Labor on, pray on, suffer on, battle on, O faithful servant of the crucified Jesus! Every day will add to your treasures in heaven.

1 Revelation 22:12.

Chapter 23

THE GREAT HYMNS

It is a remarkable fact that the finest hymns in the English language were not composed by celebrated poets; but, with the exception of those by Cowper and Montgomery, they are the productions of ministers of the Gospel and of godly women. The list of the ministers is headed by Watts, Charles Wesley, Toplady, Doddridge, Newton, Keble, Newman, Lyte, Bonar, and Ray Palmer. The list of female hymn-writers is headed by Charlotte Elliott, Mrs. Sarah F. Adams, Miss Havergall, and Mrs. Prentiss. To these may be added our blind songstress, Fanny Crosby, whose productions have not much poetic merit, and yet are sung by millions all round the globe.

A perfect hymn need not be artistically a perfect poem; much less is it a mere expression of devout spiritual experience; but it must be addressed directly to the Divine Being. The immortal hymns that never wear out are not pious self-colloquies, or sermons to our fellow-creatures; they all point upward. If my readers will run their eyes over the thirty or forty universal favorites that have stood the test of wide usage, and voice the heart sentiments of God's people in all lands, they will find that they are either metrical prayer, or metrical

praise, or both combined. Millions of pious verses have been
written; but the standard songs of solid gold could all be contained in a small booklet, and they were composed by men or
women whose genius was largely a genius for godliness.

By almost universal acclamation, the king of English hymns
is "Rock of Ages." Augustus Toplady was the son of a British
officer, and was converted by the simple, fervid sermon of an
uneducated exhorter, delivered in a barn, in Codymain, Ireland.
He became the vicar of Broad Hembury, in Devonshire, and
his zealous career, which was like that "of a race-horse, all nerve
and fire," ended at the early age of thirty-eight. He was waging
a hot doctrinal controversy with John Wesley (in which both
combatants indulged in some astonishing personalities), and
one day in March, 1776, he published in the *Gospel Magazine*
four stanzas, entitled "A living and dying Prayer for the *holiest
believer* in the world." These four hurriedly written verses are
the immortal "Rock of Ages," which Prince Albert repeated
on his dying bed, which Gladstone translated into Latin,
which are in every evangelical hymn-book, and of which it has
been truly said that "no other English hymn has laid so broad
and firm a grasp on the English speaking world." A gentleman residing among the Mendip Hills has lately claimed that
Toplady got his first idea of the imagery of the hymn while rid-
ing through a deep cleft of rocks in that neighborhood during
a thunderstorm; but I can discover no good historical foun-
dation for this singular claim. The core-idea of this sublime
production is the fervid outcry of a broken, penitent heart to
the Saviour Christ. It begins in lowly prostration before the
cross; it begs for cleansing in the atoning blood; it reaches on
to the hour when the heartstrings break in death; it sweeps
out into eternity and soars to the judgment-seat; it closes with
the glorified believer in presence of the great white Throne.

What a magnificent upward movement! I would rather be the author of this matchless prayer-song than of Milton's "Paradise Lost."

It is a curious fact that the next most popular hymn in our language should have been composed by one of the two brothers with whom Toplady had his warm conflict. I rather rejoice in this fact, for it shows how all Christian controversialists must ground arms before the cross of Christ. Charles Wesley, the greatest of Methodist singers, and Chalmers, the greatest of Presbyterian preachers, hang side by side on my study wall in loving fellowship. If ever there was a born singer it was Charles Wesley; he ate, drank, slept and dreamed of little else but making hymns. Of all his over six thousand hymns, the unquestioned masterpiece is "Jesus, lover of my soul." It is the queen of all the lays of holy love, the passionate yearning of a redeemed soul for its Redeemer. Its figures of speech vary; in one line we see a storm-tossed voyager crying out for shelter from the tempest; in another line we see a child nestling in its mother's arms; but the central thought never changes. O, how many of us in dark hours of trial have poured out our troubled hearts in these two beseeching lines,

> Leave, ah, leave me not alone,
> Still support and comfort me!

Wesley composed this superb hymn in early life, within a few months of the date of the beginning of Methodism. Many apocryphal stories have been circulated as to the origin of the hymn, such as that its author saw a bird pursued by a hawk, and that he saw a dove fly into his window, etc., etc. They only belittle the glorious thought which filled his soul when he threw himself, like the beloved disciple, on the bosom of Jesus.

Is there any American hymn that can be named after these two crown-jewels of British hymnology? Yes, there is one, and the only one that I can now think of. In the year 1830, a young teacher in a school in New York City, who had been a dry goods clerk in Boston, and had just graduated from Yale College (at the age of twenty-two), sat down one afternoon and wrote four verses, which he said were "born of my own soul." His eyes swam with tears while he wrote. Two years afterwards the young Mr. Ray Palmer was met by Lowell Mason in Boston, and asked to furnish a hymn for a new music-book soon to be issued. Palmer drew out from his pocket the four verses beginning with the words, "My faith looks up to Thee." He handed them to Mason and—thus secured his own immortality!

This beautiful hymn of the cross—inspired by the love of Jesus in his own heart—was addressed, not to his fellow-creatures, but directly to the Son of God; and, like Toplady's great hymn, it rises from before the cross of Calvary up through consecration and consolation under trials to the glories of the "ransomed"! During his long ministry, my beloved friend Palmer wrote several graceful and devout hymns; but he had struck twelve at the start. A few years before his death he officiated at a communion service in my Lafayette Avenue church in Brooklyn. While the cup was being passed to the communicants the dear old man broke out, and with tremulous voice sang his own heavenly lines,

> My faith looks up to Thee,
> Thou Lamb of Calvary,
> Saviour divine!

It was like listening to a rehearsal for the celestial choir, and the whole assembly were most deeply moved.

Next to these three absolutely perfect productions, if I were called upon to name a fourth, I would indicate Charlotte Elliott's "Just as I am, without one plea." When in frail health, she composed at her brother's, the Rev. Henry V. Elliott's house in Brighton, these exquisitely tender lines, and published them in the *Invalid's Hymn Book*. Although written by an invalid, they have, by God's blessing, made many a sick soul well. This is the hymn pre-eminently for revival meetings, and to be sung after a discourse to awakened sinners. It is a penitent's prayer in verse, and the person who can sing these words "with the spirit and the understanding" is already on the way to Jesus.

In one brief article it is impossible to discuss all the hymns that lie closest to my own heart, and which are likewise universal favorites. Each one is adapted to a particular mood of mind. At the communion table we want to sing, "When I survey the wondrous cross," or, "There is a fountain filled with blood." These were Spurgeon's favorites, and contained the keynote of his preaching. In a prayer-meeting nothing can be better than Bonar's "I heard the voice of Jesus say," or Mrs. Prentiss's "More love to Thee, O Christ!" or Perronet's "All hail the power of Jesus's name!" This last is a grand song on which to launch a meeting. For hours of bewilderment we are inclined to try Newman's wonderful lines, "Lead, kindly light!" The last two of those lines are unsurpassed for sweetness. At evening worship, what hymn can excel Keble's "Sun of my soul, Thou Saviour dear!" No missionary gathering would be complete without Bishop Heber's "From Greenland's icy mountains." Never can I forget the scene when a lovely member of my church in her dying moments repeated, with thrilling emotion, those infinitely tender lines of Henry Lyte,

"Abide with me; fast falls the eventide." It was the last of earth, and sounded like the first strain of heaven. God be praised for all these magnificent hymns. They are the marching music to which all of Christ's vast army keep step, through sunshine or storm, on their upward way to glory.

Chapter 24

OUR GOD AS A REWARDER

Among all the names and attributes of our heavenly Father, there is a very endearing one that is contained in that glorious epic of faith, the eleventh chapter of the Hebrews. We there read that God is the "rewarder of them that diligently seek Him."[1] That precious promise is linked with every earnest prayer and every act of obedience. God rewards labor. Does not every farmer act in faith when he drives his plow in springtime and drops his grain into the mellow ground? Every minister prepares his Gospel message, every Sabbath school teacher conducts the Bible lesson, and every godly parent tills the soil of the child's docile heart in the simple faith that God rewards sowing with harvests.

God rewards obedience. He enjoins upon every sinner repentance and the forsaking of his sins and the acceptance of Jesus Christ as his atoning Saviour. Every sinner that breaks off from his sins and lays hold of Jesus Christ does it on the assurance that our truth-keeping God will reward obedience. "By faith, Noah being warned of God of things not seen as yet, prepared an ark to the saving of his house."[2] An unbelieving

---

1 Hebrews 11:6.
2 Hebrews 11:7.

generation hooted, no doubt, at the "fanatic" who was wasting his time and money on that unwieldy vessel.

God rewards believing prayer for right things, when it is offered in a submissive spirit. "Ask, and ye shall receive; seek, and ye shall find."[1] Humble, childlike faith creates a condition of things in which it is wise and right for God to grant what might otherwise be denied. We grasp the blessed truth that He hears prayer, and gives the best answer to prayer in His own time and way; upon these two facts we plant our knees when we bow down before Him. O, the long, long trials to which we are often subjected while our loving Father is testing our faith and giving it more vigor and volume!

Godly wives are often left to press their earnest petitions through months and years before the answer comes in the work of the converting Spirit. There was an excellent woman in my congregation who was for a long time anxious for the conversion of her husband. She endeavored to make her own Christian life very attractive to him—a very important point, too often neglected. On a certain Sabbath she shut herself up and spent much of the day in beseeching prayers that God would touch her husband's heart. She said nothing to her husband, but took the case straight up to the throne of grace. The next day when she opened her Bible to conduct family worship, according to her custom, he came and took the book out of her hands and said, "Wifey, it is about time that I did this," and he read the chapter himself. Before the week was over he was praying himself, and at the next communion he united with our church.

Verily, God is a rewarder of them that diligently seek Him. That praying Hannah who said, "The grief of my heart is that of all of my six children not one loves Jesus," was not satisfied

1 See Matthew 7:7.

that it should be so. She continued her fervent supplications until five of them were converted during a revival. They all united in a day of fasting and prayer for the sixth daughter, and she was soon rejoicing in Christ. The victory that overcame in that case was a faith that would not be denied.

Sometimes the prayers of parents are answered long after the lips that breathed them are molded into dust. When a certain Captain K—— sailed on his last sea voyage he left a prayer for his little boy written out and deposited in an oaken chest. After his death at sea his widow locked up his chest, and when she was on her dying bed she gave the key to their son. He grew up a licentious and dissolute man. When he had reached middle life he determined to open that chest, out of mere curiosity. He found in it a paper, on the outside of which was written, "The prayer of M—— K—— for his wife and child." He read the prayer, put it back in the chest, but could not lock it out of his troubled heart. It burned there like a live coal. He became so distressed that the woman with whom he was living as his mistress thought he was becoming deranged. He broke down in penitence, cried to God for mercy, and, making the woman his legal wife, began a new life of prayer and obedience to God's commandments. And so God proved to be the rewarder of a faith that had been hidden away in a secret place a half a century before! I have no doubt that among the blessed surprises in eternity will be the triumphs of many a believer's trusting prayers.

Chapter 25

LIGHT AT EVENING TIME

I once ascended Mount Washington with a party of friends on horseback, and we were overtaken by a violent storm, followed by a blinding mist. After our rough scramble over slippery rocks, it was a woeful disappointment to find, on our arrival at the "Tip-top House," that we could not see any object two rods from the door. But late in the afternoon the clouds began to roll away, and one mountain after another revealed itself to our view. At length the sun burst forth, and overarched the valley of the Saco with a gorgeous rainbow; we came out and gazed upon the magnificent panorama with wondering delight, and, as the rays of the setting sun kindled every mountain peak with gold, we all exclaimed, "At evening time it shall be light!"

My experience on that mountain top is a striking illustration of the experiences of God's people in all ages. Faith has had its steep Hills of Difficulty to climb, and often through blinding mists and hurtling storms. Unbelief says, "halt," and despair cries, "go back!" But hope keeps up its steady, cheery song, "It will be better further on." The poor old patriarch Jacob wails out that all things are against him, and that he will go down to his grave mourning. Wait a little. Yonder comes the caravan from Egypt laden with sacks of corn and bringing the good tidings that Joseph is the prime minister of Pharaoh's government! To the astonished old man at evening time it is light!

The office of faith is to cling to the fact that behind all clouds, however thick, and all storms, however fierce, God is on the throne. It is the office of hope to look for the clearing of the clouds in God's good time. If we had no storms we should never appreciate the blue skies; the trials of the tempest are the preparation for the afterglow of the sunshine. We ought never to think it strange that difficulties confront us, or trials assail us; for this is but a part of our discipline, and in the end all things work for good to them whom God loveth and who trust Him. It is according to God's established economy that we should be exposed to temptations, and often to trials which threaten to drive us to despair. All this is to teach us our dependence upon Him. No climb of duty is so high, so steep, or so hard, but God is standing at the top! No honest work for Him is ever entirely in vain. I will go farther and affirm that no honest prayer was ever yet uttered in the right spirit, and failed to get some answer; if not the thing asked for, yet some other good thing has been granted. And oh, how often God surprises us after a long day of struggles and discouragements by a glorious outburst of light at evening time!

There is hardly any passage in our Bible that is more full of encouragement to faithful ministers and teachers and parents, and to all who are toiling in Christian enterprises than this very text that suggests this article. Things easily done are generally of small value; it is the costly undertakings that counts. From the days of Bethlehem, Gethsemane and Calvary the history of the Christian Church has been: conflict before victory, labor before reward, shadow before sunlight. When Europe had long been enshrouded in the "dark ages" Martin Luther seized the trumpet of the Saxon tongue and blew a blast that rang from Rome to the Orkneys. I well remember when my friend John G. Whittier was threatened with personal violence on account of his advocacy of negro emancipation; the grand old poet lived to sing the triumph of union and liberty. I could recall incidents in my own experience that illustrate how, after dark days of discouragement, at evening time it was light. In my first pastoral charge of a small church, the discouragements were so great that I was under a strong temptation to abandon the difficult field of labor entirely. Suddenly there came the most remarkable outpouring of the Holy Spirit that I have ever witnessed during my whole ministry! That revival was worth more to me than any year in the theological seminary.

This beautiful passage of the bright eventide is finely descriptive of a Christian old age. Some people have a pitiful dread of growing old, and count it a disgrace. They possibly think that if the line in their family Bible that records the day of their birth were subjected to the fashionable process of the "higher criticism," it might prove to be erroneous! But if life is spent in God's service its later years may be well described in the quaint Scotch version of the 92ND Psalm:

> And in old age when others fade,
> They fruit still forth shall bring;
> They shall be fat, and full of sap,
> And aye be flourishing.

The October of life frequently yields its richest and ripest fruitage. The Rev. Dr. Richard S. Storrs delivered his most magnificent sermons and addresses after he had passed threescore. The most majestic and thrilling burst of eloquence that ever flowed from Gladstone's lips was that appeal for bleeding Armenia, when his life-clock had already struck eighty-six! Why should not the Indian summers of a well-spent life show every leaf on the tree blazing with ruddy gold? That noble old Christian philanthropist, William Wilberforce (who had suffered severe pecuniary losses), wrote in his diary, "I sometimes understand why my life has been spared so long. It is to prove that I can be just as happy without my fortune as when I possessed it. Sailors, it is said, when on a voyage at sea, drink to 'friends astern' until they get half away across, and then to 'friends ahead' for the rest of the voyage. With me it has been friends ahead for many a year." Wilberforce was not the only veteran Christian who got glimpses of the friends ahead in the bright afterglow of life.

If it is true that the old age of a faithful follower of Christ exhibits the light at eventide, still more impressively does this often apply to his or her dying bed. During my active pastorate I sometimes get better sermons from my people than I ever gave to them. I recall now a most touching and sublime scene that I once witnessed in the death-chamber of a noble woman who had suffered for many months from an excruciating malady. The end was drawing near. She seemed to be catching a fore-gleam of the glory that awaited her. With tremulous tones she began to repeat Henry Lyte's matchless hymn, "Abide with me, fast falls the eventide." One line after another was feebly repeated until, with a rapturous sweetness, she exclaimed:

> Hold Thou Thy Cross before my closing eyes,
> Shine through the gloom and point me to the skies,
> Heaven's morning breaks, and earth's vain shadows flee,
> In life, in death, O Lord, abide with me.

As I came away from that room, which had been as the vestibule of heaven, I understood how the "light at eventime" could be only a flashing forth of the overwhelming glory that plays forever around the throne of God!

Made in the USA
Columbia, SC
13 December 2022

72629612R00069